WASSUP WITH A BLACK BOYS SITTING IN THE PRINCIPAL'S OFFICE?

An Examination of Detrimental Teacher Interactions & School Practices

Dr. Rashad Anderson

Printed in the United States of America, 2019

48 Hour Books
2249 14th St. SW
Akron OH 44314

ISBN-13: 978-0-578-51702-5
ISBN-10: 0-578-51702-7

Quantity sales. Special discounts are available on quantity purchases by corporations, associations, and others. For details, contact the author at andersonrashad@hotmail.com

Also available on Amazon

This book is dedicated to the little Black boy wonders who let me in their lives for this endeavor. When I looked at you all, I saw myself. I had no choice but to stop and listen to your stories. I pray your stories illuminates the path for others.

SPECIAL THANKS

I first would like to thank God, who instilled in me a dream and paved the way for me to do this work. To my late mother Teresa and my father Benjamin, I can never truly express the extent of my love and gratitude for your unwavering support & tutelage throughout the years. From holding my hand as you both walked me to my first day of pre-school, to helping me move in my room as college freshman, to the present, you have always been right by my side and your sacrifices, advice, and love are priceless to me. Mom, I know you are watching down on me from heaven. To my brother Desmond, thank you for being my champion throughout the years.

To my supportive colleagues at Carolina Elementary, thank you for being my family away from home. Special thanks to my second mom, Gwendolyn Anderson, Vincent Sanders, and Gloria Jenkins. Your motivation, support, and belief in me aided me throughout this journey in writing this book.

To all my brothers of the Call Me MiSTER program, especially to my little brothers of the SC State University Cohort, thank you for being a constant source of love, focus, and motivation. Particular thanks goes to Samuel Murray & Andrew Bratton for helping me spread this research across the United States. Also, special thanks to Lemanuel Chandler, Rashad Paige, Lawrence Ochieng, Winston Holton, and Dr. Roy Jones for teaching me to be unafraid of the greatness I had inside of me.

To my countless fraternity brothers of Alpha Phi Alpha Fraternity and Phi Mu Alpha Sinfonia Fraternity, I thank you for the unwavering brotherhood, support, and motivation throughout the years, especially my line brother Albert Shuler.

And last but not least, I would like to thank anyone that kept my in prayer—you kept me personally and spiritually lifted throughout this rollercoaster of a journey of completing this study & writing this book.

5

Chapter Seven: Specific Acts of Marginalization Towards Black Males

SECTION 3: BRINGING IT ALL TOGETHER

SECTION 1

**Chapter One:
"The Why"**

I am invisible. Misunderstood, simply because people refuse to see me. Like the bodiless heads you see sometimes in circus sideshows, it is as though I have been surrounded by mirrors of hard, distorting glass. When they approach me they see only my surroundings, themselves, or fragments of their imagination—indeed, everything and anything except me (Ellison, 1952).

Every time I walked in the front office I asked myself, "Why is there always a long line of Black boys sitting, waiting to be seen by the principal?" As a first-year music teacher in a rural elementary school in South Carolina, I found myself perplexed and deeply impacted by what I observed within the first few weeks of school. As a new teacher I was immediately schooled on the unofficial practices and culture of the school that I was employed. One of those unofficial practices at my school dealt with a classroom management technique. I often noticed that if teachers had a problem with a student in their class, they would normally send that student out to sit in the hallway to await permission to re-enter the classroom. I soon realized that at any point during the day, if I opened my classroom door, as I looked to my left & right, as far as the eye could see, all I saw was Black boys standing and sitting in the hallway after having been sent out of class. It was in the hallway that I would see these young Black male students laying down, staring up at the ceiling, fidgeting with items in their pocket, or staring at their classmates thru the classroom door window, all while instruction continued without them.

7

I would then frequently visit the main office on my lunch break to use the staff microwave only to be greeted with an office full of Black boys waiting to be seen by our administrators or guidance staff. When I walked into the office, most of the boy's faces would light up and they reached their hands out to give me a handshake or try to explain to me why they were sitting in the office. Then I begin noticing that during my playground duty a disproportionate number of Black male students standing by the fence as a punishment during recess or sitting on the pavement writing hundreds of "I will behave in class" type sentences as a punishment. Several of my Black male peers who also just began their teaching careers in other school districts corroborated and shared similar observations and experiences with Black male students at their schools. I quickly realized, the problems of Black males in schools was happening all around.

Within the first three months of being a teacher, I clearly saw an alarming, but confusing problem. You see, in our faculty meetings, teachers were often presented with data concerning the achievement gap of our Black student population. At Carolina Elementary school, the African American demographic scored the lowest on all subject areas on the state tests. Several district personnel that led our professional development even drilled the importance of "failure is not an option for ANY student" and that every teacher must focus on maximizing instructional time. In fact, it should have been blatantly obvious that Carolina Elementary had a lot of work to do when it came to the education of Black male students. This was actually one of the first facts that I learned from the Asst. Superintendent that recruited me during a teacher recruitment fair. As a recent HBCU graduate and member of the nationally acclaimed Call Me MiSTER program (a teacher leadership program that recruits, trains, & places more Black males to be elementary teachers), I was particularly excited to be the very first Black male teacher Carolina Elementary ever had.

I remember sitting in this professional development meeting listening to the solemn instructions from our district Curriculum Coordinator and beginning to think in my head, "What the hell is going on here?!" I knew that I was a first-year teacher but things just didn't make sense! If failure was not an option for ANY student and teachers were mandated to maximize instructional time, then why was it so normalized at Carolina Elementary to see Black male students sitting in the hallway or principal's office while lessons were going on? I guess our Curriculum Coordinator's mandate referred to all students, except, Black males.

As a graduate of a teacher education program at an HBCU, combined with my own experience of being a Black male going thru school, I was frequently exposed to a wide variety of literature, scholars, and experiences that exposed the negative schooling practices and trends in regards to Black male students; however, as fledging educator it was quite surreal for me to see this phenomenon in first person at this magnitude. Even more disconcerting for me was the level of indifference and indolence teachers had in addressing what seemed to be, an obvious problem concerning the schooling and education of Black male students in public schools. My experiences left me with an urge to do something about this silent, strangely accepted, crisis.

Four months after starting my teaching career, I went to my principal with an idea. I asked my principal for permission to start up a mentoring program for the young Black males in the school. I wanted to begin the program with thirty students the principal selected that had the most discipline problems and/or the most likely to be retained in their current grade level. Two weeks after the initial conversation with my principal, my male mentoring program Brothers' Keeper was formed. It was then that the inspiration for this book came about.

I began each meeting with the 30 precocious young boys in my mentoring program where we all sat on the floor in a circle that we called the "Brotherhood Circle" --where every member spoke about anything that was frustrating, exciting, or going on in their lives. After two weeks of consecutive powerful interactions between the students and I in the "Brotherhood Circle", it became clear to me what direction I would complete my yearlong educational research study on which initially began as a dissertation study. I was surprised and moved by the stirring stories of despair and frustration by these young boys. Perhaps even more powerful to me was that the Brotherhood circle began to evolve into a group therapy session where other members encouraged and coached each other on how to navigate and persist in the minefield terrain known as Carolina Elementary. The teaching profession had to hear what these students had to say about school and their experiences, thus the purpose of this book.

Chapter Two:

The Background Story of this Research

The purpose of my yearlong study was to examine how five pre-adolescent African American males from a rural elementary school in South Carolina, who have been identified as "at-risk," articulated both their current and past schooling experiences. I was interested in examining what their experiences revealed about their interactions and engagements with their teachers and other practices within/without the school in which they may have experienced marginalization.

I must admit I was particularly nervous at first about approaching my principal and the superintendent about conducting this study at the same school and district that I was employed. Prayerfully, both my principal and superintendent were extremely supportive and anxious to see the results from this study. I was granted full access to the student and district data that I needed and was even periodically given a substitute teacher to relieve me of my teaching duties so that I could interview students, parents, and teachers and conduct observations.

Though I religiously maintained my meeting schedule with my mentoring program and tried my best to forge deep and meaningful relationships with all 30 mentees daily in my program, I must admit that the five students that I used as participants in this study grew very near and dear to my heart beyond all my other mentees. For over a year I tried to entrench myself in "their shoes." I was able to spend time and conduct a series of interviews with their current and past teachers, older friends of the participants' families, and even the parents/guardians of the five students. In a way, I soon became a neutral sounding bar for all of these persons involved in these young people lives.

I approached this research with a unique positionality. A qualitative researcher serves as an instrument for data collection (Creswell, 2007; Harper & Gasman, 2008). As such, it is important to address who I am in relation to this study. I am a Black male teacher in my early thirties. At the time this study was conducted, I had taught in public schools for over four years and had extensive experience working with programs and orphanages that serve at-risk males of all ethnicities. Within my personal life, though I would describe my own schooling experiences as generally positive, I have several male family members who have experienced school in turbulent terms. Perhaps the most salient refrain I consistently observed or has been shared with me by students, mentees, and family members, is the dynamic between the student and the teacher is critically important. The narratives of almost all of these males seem to contain an account of the student feeling as though the teacher did not like or value them, ultimately influencing the way they felt about, engaged in, and valued school.

As a Black man, a teacher, and a researcher, I carry various levels of consciousness in regards to the systemic issues plaguing boys of color in our public schools. Knowing each of their stories reflects multiple influences that have shaped their schooling experiences, I am not an advocate for totally placing the blame for these young males' failure on the school or the educators in charge.

As an educator, one that taught each of the five participants at some point during their tenure at Carolina Elementary, I was well aware of the immense pressure to increase test scores with limited resources and a room full of diverse learners, abilities, and behaviors. However, because of my insider position as an educator, coupled with personal experiences as a former student, I also had seen multiple, rich occurrences, interactions, policies, and situations in which teachers engaged that negatively impacted Black males within the schooling environment. Thus as a researcher, I approached this study as an opportunity to partner with participants to share their voices and ideas in order to improve the journeys and the spaces they occupy in school. While I recognize that I was unable to remove myself from these identities as I conducted this study, I also felt as though my identities provided me a level of intimacy with my study and participants.

Chapter Three:

The Silent Crisis in U.S. Public Schools

There is a sobering reality when it comes to the schooling of African American males in the United States. In virtually all categories, African American males experience school quite differently than any other population. Despite the supposed promise of educational policies such as No Child Left Behind, a multitude of school reform efforts, increased standardization in schools, the promulgation of high stakes testing, the influx of charter schools nationwide, the surge of districts being taken over by states, and the growing corporate presence to oversee schools, there still remains a large segment of students who fail to gain access to high-quality education (Darling-Hammond, 2006, 2010; Howard, 2010). Of this segment of students, African American males are one of the more academically and socially marginalized groups in U. S. schools (Anderson, 2008; Noguera, 2008). On all of the indicators of academic achievement, educational attainment, and school success, African-American males are noticeably distinguished from other segments of the American population by their consistent clustering at the bottom (Schott, 2010). With some exceptions, these patterns exist in urban, suburban, and rural school districts throughout the United States and are influenced by political, social and economic factors.

While African American males currently make up 17% of the total school population, they account for 32% of the suspensions and 30% of all expulsions (Milner, 2006; Noguera, 2002; School to Prison Pipeline, 2006; U.S. Census Bureau 2012). Black boys are 2.5 times less likely to be enrolled in gifted and talented programs and conversely, make up

14

80% of the U.S. students classified as special needs (Noguera, 2002). In particular, African-American boys perform poorly compared with White boys or African-American girls in different educational outcomes.

According to Kunjufu (2004), Black male students mentally and emotionally dropout of school around the fourth grade if they are not caught early and redirected in the area of academic studies, character, and moral development. As a result of teachers' disproportionate referral of Black boys for disciplinary sanctions, young Black male students may have an increase in discipline problems and manifest learning disabilities or consistently struggle academically (Kunjufu, 2004). Data from 2003 to 2009 indicate that by fourth grade, African-American boys in public schools score about thirty points lower in reading than White boys, and this gap remains at eighth grade. Research also demonstrates a similar trend in mathematics achievement (National Assessment of Educational Progress, 2009; U.S. Department of Education, 2014).

In 2009, the average SAT scores for Black males were lower than those for White males in critical reading, mathematics, and writing. The gap between SAT scores for White and Black students was 104 points in critical reading, 120 points in mathematics, and 99 points in writing (Casserly, Lewis, Horwitz, Simon & Uzzell, 2010). The U.S. Department of Education (2005) also claimed African-American boys also lag behind their African American female counterparts. While girls in general perform better in K-12 and college than boys, gender differences among African-American groups are larger than among other groups.

The National Assessment of Educational Progress (2009) reported Black students in economically disadvantaged communities are about four years behind White students living in similar communities by the time they reach 12th grade. The NAEP (2009) also reported

African American and Hispanic students are more likely to drop out of high school than their White peers. Data from the Schott Report (2010) on Public Education and Black males indicated that, in 2009-10, the national graduation rate for Black male students was 52%. In some major cities such as Chicago and New York the dropout rate is as high as 70% (Riddick, 2009), while the graduation rate for White males was 78%. The year 2010 was also the first year more than half of the nation's Black males in 12th grade graduated with regular diplomas within a four-year period. The U.S. schooling system has only decreased the national Black/White male graduation gap by 3 percentage points over the last decade (Schott, 2010).

Thus, these statistics re-illuminate a familiar problem within our U.S. educational system, the achievement gap. The achievement gap is defined by the Teaching Commission (2011) as the troubling academic performance gap between African American and Hispanic students in comparison with their White peers. Despite the awareness of this achievement gap, many still continue to suffer from poor school achievement, school failure, high rates of educational drop out, low college enrollment, over-representation in special education classes, and low standardized tests scores, reflecting an enveloping problem of educational underachievement among African Americans (Riddick, 2009).

While the achievement gap narrowed considerably through the late 1980s, particularly between Blacks and Whites, progress at better meeting the needs of all students since then has been marginal. The achievement gap, or as Ladson Billings (2006) redirects, the education debt for African American students, especially males, remains one of the most pressing problems in education. Education Commission of the States (2014) identified a variety of factors that appear related to the achievement gap — students' racial and/or economic background, their parents' education level, their access to high-quality preschool instruction, school funding, peer influences, teachers' expectations, and curricular and instructional quality. Since the daily interactions and nuances that take place in the classroom and school can be one of the greatest factors contributing to the achievement gap (Tyre, 2008), there is strong need to further examine and understand what students, particularly pre-adolescent Black males, have to say about their schooling experiences that might influence them to devalue and/or disengage from school at such a young age.

While examining the effect of teachers' biases and interactions on Black male students' social and academic success has been the subject of some scholars investigations (Davis, 2003; Davis & Jordan, 1995; Thomas & Stevenson, 2009; Noguera, 2002), these studies are usually centered on the researchers' observation and analysis of these interactions and their implications for Black male students. As Toldson (2013) noted, far too often everyone other than Black males have offered commentary, analysis, and narrative of their experience. The African proverb fitting here is, "Do not let the lion tell the giraffe's story." Black males' accounts of their school experiences are marginally represented in social science research. It is even more rare to encounter elementary age Black males' experiences in social science research.

Howard (2001) suggested one of the glaring absences of much of the research associated with African American males is it has not included first-hand, detailed accounts from African American males about the roles they believe power, race, and racism play in their schooling experiences. The literature that does include first-hand accounts from African American males almost always focused exclusively on high school age students. By examining the education debt through the lens of pre-adolescent males, I solicited rarely documented experiences about the ways they perceive, and what they believe about school.

17

SECTION TWO

Chapter Four:

Background of Students & School

Section two of this book "re-presents" the data collected from the participants organized around reoccurring themes that I found to persist over the course of this study. I begin this chapter by providing brief descriptions of the five young African American boys (participants) who shared their schooling experiences for this study. All of the names of the participants, faculty, staff, or any other persons mentioned or included in this study is protected through the use of pseudonyms. These descriptions are followed by a "re-presentation" of the data, organized around themes that correspond to each of the major patterns I found during the course of this study. These themes are organized under the three descriptors, school practices, teacher interactions, & acts of marginalization towards Black males. Each theme under these descriptors illustrates both similar and contrasting beliefs expressed by the students, as well as their perceptions of and experiences in school.

I begin each thematic section with data that best exemplified how the participants conceptualized and articulated the topic, followed by my interpretation of the data. Occasionally, I include images of various artifacts under the subheadings (office referrals, class documents, behavior charts, memos, files, etc.) that provide an alternative way of representing the participants' schooling experiences and stories.

Description of the Research Site: Carolina Elementary

Carolina Elementary is one of the largest elementary schools in southwest South Carolina. The facility sits between a large cotton field and a pasture of roaming cows, goats, and waterfowl. Carolina Elementary is about 10 miles outside the main city radius were several colleges and universities are located. The facility is a little over 20 years old and is kept in great condition. The floors are nicely shined and each grade level's hallway is decorated according to a theme such as the Wild West, the ocean or the jungle. Several art murals, students' work, and decorated bulletin boards adorn the walls in the halls, in the cafeteria, in the library and in the main offices. At the time of this study the walls on each hallway were covered with a recent school-wide art project called, "What Is Your beauty." Every artwork featured a skinny, White female, with long blond hair. Not one male, body type or other ethnicity was featured.

Carolina Elementary is a Title 1 School, meaning that a high percentage of the students are considered to live in low-income households. Nearly 84% of Carolina Elementary students are eligible for free or reduced lunch. Approximately 613 students attend Carolina Elementary. They are bussed in from four small communities, all within a 20-mile radius of the school. The gender demographic of the student body is almost perfectly balanced; 307 students are female and 306 students are male. The racial demographic of the student body is as follows: a) White students makes up 50%, b) African-American students makes up 45%, c) Multiracial students make up 3%, and d) students identifies as other makes up 2% of the student body. Currently 111 African American male students out of 613 students attend Carolina Elementary, accounting for 18% of the student population.

Carolina Elementary employs 31 classroom teachers. Twenty-eight of the classroom teachers are females with the remaining three being male including myself. The racial demographic of the 31 classroom teachers are 20 White female teachers, 7 female African American teachers, 1 Asian female teacher, 2 African American male teachers, and 1 White male teacher. All students belong to a homeroom class and throughout the day, rotate between five teachers to receive instruction in English Language Arts (ELA), math, science, social studies and a related arts class (art, music, physical education or media center). In my observations, homeroom classes with high percentages of African American students, particularly African American males, are remedial in nature and are taught by teachers within the school who have a reputation of being strict disciplinarians. Homeroom classes that offer more rigorous curricula, populated by students expected to enroll in the fifth grade Gifted and Talented Education program (GATE), have the least amount of African American students and are all taught by teachers who serve as their grade level chairpersons with reputations for having high test scores.

In the 2013-14 school year five of the district's elementary and secondary schools scored an F rating on the Federal Accountability System including Carolina Elementary. The graduation rate for the school district is 78%. The graduation rate for African American males in the district is 46%. The school offers a Gifted and Talented Education program (GATE) with 32 students enrolled and receiving services. Out of those 32 students, 2 are African American males, 1 African American female, 19 White female, 1 Hispanic female, and 9 are White males. The school also serves 113 students in a special education program. Out of the 113 students in the special education program, 67 students are African American males. On the schools report card, African American males are the only student demographic who did not meet any of the academic subjects tested on the State's standardized test.

Carolina Elementary also has the highest suspension rates when compared with the other three elementary schools in the district. In the 2012-2013 school year Carolina recorded 237 suspensions. Boys made up 204 of those suspensions and girls made up 33 suspensions. Of those 237 suspensions, 170 of those suspended were African American students, 56 were White students, 11 were identified as other, and 2 were multiracial students. Twelve out of the twelve students that Carolina Elementary placed in the district's alternative school were all African American students. Ten out of the 11 students expelled from Carolina Elementary were African American students.

Participant Descriptions

Participant 1-Hakeem. Hakeem is in the fifth grade and lives with his parents, three siblings, and nephew in a neighborhood not far from the school. Hakeem's mother works as a clerk at the local grocery store and his father works part time for a local landscaping business. Hakeem is the third of four children. When Hakeem was in the second grade he and his siblings were taken from their parents' custody and placed in foster care after his parents were found guilty of abusing drugs. After his parents served time in jail and went through a lengthy rehabilitation period, Hakeem and his siblings returned to his parents' custody a few months before he started the fourth grade. Hakeem's father visits the school occasionally to check in on him and his daughter who also attends Carolina Elementary.

When Hakeem was in the fourth grade his older brother in the 11th grade was incarcerated after being found guilty of selling marijuana. In that same year his older sister, then in the seventh grade, became pregnant and dropped out of school for a period of time. Hakeem's younger sister, now in the fourth grade, has maintained straight A's since the first grade. Hakeem has been a student at Carolina Elementary for two years after having been expelled from his previous school district in his third grade year for excessive discipline referrals. A review of Hakeem's disciplinary records from his previous school district reveals a vast difference in the types of referrals he received such as having sagging pants, fighting, having a "bad attitude", using poor manners, stealing, consistently coming to school without materials, and bullying other students.

21

In the fourth grade Hakeem was suspended in the spring for three weeks and placed on probation from Carolina Elementary after bringing his older brother's pellet gun to school in his bookbag. Hakeem has had four discipline referrals since then. Hakeem was recently changed to a new homeroom teacher in the middle of the year after three parents, two who are officials in the school's Parent Teacher Organization (P.T.O.), made allegations to school personnel that Hakeem made physical threats to their child and were uncomfortable with having him remain in the same homeroom class as their child. Hakeem's new homeroom teacher describes him as a typical boy. She said:

> I'm shocked about the things I've heard he's done. He's quiet and one of my smartest kids. I think people take a look at Hakeem and immediately assume he is another prison case kid because of his background and the way he looks. If you treat any child like that I wouldn't blame them for acting out. Every child deserves some tender love and care if you ask me. The only time I ever really have a problem with him is like when he gets bored in class or someone agitates him. I can't say I've ever seen him instigate problems with kids as some of his other teachers may say.

In contrast, a school staff member also describes Hakeem as a "ticking time bomb waiting to go off." This staff member claims:

> Hakeem is sneaky. Don't let him fool you. He's smart and he knows he's on his last leg in this school district. Hakeem terrorizes the other students and they are afraid of him. He's just more sneakery now about how he does it. I hate to say this about a child but he acts like some kind of thug. I feel sorry for him because

that's probably the way he had to grow up living in his kind of household but its still not fair to have him in the class with other children that come to school to learn.

Hakeem's academic records reveal that he has never had problems in the classroom in terms of academic achievement. In fact, Hakeem made straight A's one quarter in the second grade. Currently, Hakeem's lowest grade is an 74 in math. He has at least an 83 or higher in all his other subjects. His math teacher remarks that he is "more focused on acting like a thug than doing his work and being a normal student. If he did he would have better grades. Hakeem doesn't care about school and when I call his parents they act like they don't care either. I've done all I can to help him." Hakeem describes himself as a "serious kid that likes to hunt and be with (his) friends."

Participant 2-Samuel. Samuel describes himself as a kid who is smart, good in music, and loves going to church. Samuel is in the fifth grade again after being retained because of his low grades from the last school year. Samuel is noted by his teachers for "loving to talk your head off" and having a great singing voice. Samuel lives with grandmother and aunt. He is the only child. When Samuel was three his mother was killed in a car accident and his father was soon imprisoned thereafter for reasons unknown. His aunt, now disabled, was a prominent evangelist in the area before she retired many years ago. His grandmother still works as minister of music at a local church and still teaches organ lessons in her spare time. Samuel has been playing the organ and singing in the church choir since he was four years old. Samuel sings lead in the school choir and has won the school talent show every year since he's been at Carolina Elementary.

Throughout Samuel's tenure from kindergarten to the fifth grade he's been referred to the office a total of 11 times. Samuel's school file indicated that his referrals dealt mostly with academics more so than misbehavior such as not completing work, coming to class unprepared or refusing to do school work. Samuel is failing three of his major subjects this school term and could possibly be retained in the 5th grade for a third time if his grades do not improve. In the second grade Samuel was tested for special education but did not qualify for services.

Samuel records indicated that he struggled much throughout elementary school with the exception of his fourth grade year when he was three points away from making the A/B honor roll. Interestingly, Samuel's fourth grade year was his first time having a major subject teacher who is a Black male. Currently, Samuel's science teacher remarks that, "he is a wise kid. You can tell that by the way he can carries a conversation but for some reason he rarely does his work and when he does do it, it's usually wrong."

Samuel's grandmother remarks that:

> I do all I can to make sure that boy stay top of that school work.
> I go to the parent conferences and I check his agenda and
> homework. Now I'm a old woman so I couldn't tell you if he
> does his work right or not but I can tell you that it at least be
> something on the paper. I don't really know how much more I
> can do to help him. School has changed a whole lot since I was
> in it. Child it seem like you need a college degree now days to
> send your chillun to school and do good.

Participant 3-Quincy. Quincy is in the fourth grade and noticeably, much taller than most other fifth graders. Quincy lives with his godparents and godbrother. Quincy's godmother is a registered nurse at the local hospital and his godfather is football coach at a nearby high school. Quincy's godparents have three sons, one in high school, one in college and one in the marines. Quincy's godbrothers are prominent members in their community after their successful tenure in high school and college football. Quincy is the quarterback for his little league football team.

In the middle of Quincy's third grade year his mother granted custody of Quincy to his godparents after the school district threatened to expel him. Quincy had already been expelled once from a school district in Pennsylvania in the second grade. Quincy is the second oldest of six children and the only boy. Quincy's godparents initially met Quincy's mother at church when she was pregnant and many years later, began babysitting Quincy when he was a small child. When he was four, Quincy's godparents took him in for about a year when his mother moved from South Carolina to Pennsylvania to find work. Quincy's godmother stated:

> We have kept Quincy off and on for many years and everytime his
> mom would send for him in whatever state she was in at the
> moment and uproot him once he got settled with us. That's when
> the school problems really started to begin. When things got real
> bad she would send him back down here with us for awhile. From
> kindergarten to about third grade that boy went back and forth
> between school in South Carolina with us and out of the state with
> her. Finally I think when she realized when he was about to get
> expelled again that it was best for him to just come live with us
> permanently. We don't mind; we love him like our own. He know
> we don't play that foolishness in school in this house!

Last school year Quincy had more office referrals than any other student in the school. The District's Board of Education summoned him to consider expelling him because of his long track record of office referrals. In my review of his disciplinary file, it appeared as though he was often referred to the office due to defiance to teachers, inappropriate language to school staff and peers, bullying and stealing. Quincy made history in the district by being the only third grader to ever be considered for expulsion with over 40 office referrals. Part of the reason for Quincy's excessive amount of office referrals derived from his homeroom teacher's decision to actively encourage other teachers to write him up for any infractions in order to create "a paper trail" to quickly have enough evidence for the Board to expel him from the school district. When I asked Quincy's third grade math teacher to recall her experience with Quincy from last year she said:

> In my 23 years of teaching I've never encountered a child like Quincy. I hate to say it but most days he was like a demon child that made my life a living hell! He bullied the other children, lied to me, disrespected me, and even stole from me. He needed help that our school simply couldn't provide. And the crazy thing is that that boy could easily make straight A's if he wanted. He's super intelligent. Last year he just decided to use his wit to get him in the office more than a classroom. He really needed to be either in an alternative school or another school more fitted for him.

Since moving in with his godparents Quincy's office referral rate has decreased dramatically since his third-grade year. This school term Quincy has averaged a total of nine office referrals in nine weeks, two which resulted in him being suspended from school. Though his referral rate has decreased substantially from last year, Quincy is only three office

26

referrals away from having the most referrals in his current grade level. Quincy's current homeroom teacher, who also attends the same church as Quincy and his godparents, said:

> Other teachers act like they afraid of him. Quincy 'bout as tall as most teachers in the building so I think that adds to their fear or perception of him as an adult. We adults got to remember that Quincy is a child and he deserves to be treated no different than any other 4th grader no matter how tall he is. Bump a reputation. See when he comes to my room he does his work, he has his fun but still is respectful and good. No matter how old you get you got to remember these are children though. They aint meant to sit in desks all day and never make a mistake. He know I love em but I don't play no foolishness. Once you build a relationship with Quincy he will do anything you ask of him pretty much. That don't mean you never chastise him if he wrong, it just means he knows while you fussing that you still love him to death just like he was your own son.

Quincy describes himself as a cute, smart student who loves sports and hates school. He said he acts the way he does because others either entice him to do so or he feels as though his teachers do not like him. Quincy mentioned in one of his journal entries for this study that, "If somebody bothers me or I feel like they don't like me I get real mad and shut down."

Participant 4-David. David is rather short for his age group, animated, and loves to laugh. In David's autobiography he describes himself as "funny, smart, and someone who

27

likes to share." David is in the third grade and lives with both of his parents. David is an only child. David's father is a retired military officer and his mom is an insurance agent. David father visits the school every week to observe him in class or to volunteer for several of the school events and activities. This is David's first year at Carolina Elementary and he was recently referred to the school's intervention team because of his low grades in math, science, and social studies. David has also been referred to the office four times within his five months of attending Carolina Elementary.

David is one of two African American males in his class. Both boys are failing multiple subjects and are the only students in the class who have received office referrals thus far. David exclaims that he loves school because of his friends but hates his teacher because she is very mean to him. David says, "I always get in trouble and told that I'm bad and she always think it's me doing something wrong but she never says anything to anybody else." A review of David's disciplinary file indicate that he has been written up for "not completing homework", "not participating in class", "having a bad attitude with the teacher and his peers", and "excessive talking during class." One of the African American school officials expressed frustration with David's homeroom teacher (a White female) that made the referrals. She mentioned:

> Every year we have the same problem with his teacher, Black
> boys! Black boys that never had problems in school seem to always
> start having severe problems once they get to her. I mean the
> things she writes these boys up makes no sense! She said
> something to me in the hallway that a few days ago David gave her
> this look that could kill. You know she sent him to me for that?
> What the hell!

When I asked David's homeroom teacher to explain to me how he was doing in her class, she exclaimed:

> That little boy frustrates me so! It's not that he's stupid at all.
> He's so smart. I mean he really is. He passed 9 out of 11 of his
> accelerated reader tests! He does well when he wants to. He just
> always decides to goof off, not do work, or catch horrible little
> attitudes with me. I'm not having it.

I asked David's father how he feels about the way David is doing in school. He responded by saying:

> I come up here so much because I was trying to figure out was it
> something that we're doing wrong at home or is it the school.
> We've never had this problem with him before. At first I use to
> get on David so much about doing so bad in school but now I
> really think she's [David's homeroom teacher] racist. There's
> been several times she has tried to demean me or talk over my
> head in conferences so I can imagine what my son goes through.
> The new quarter, my wife and I will be requesting to put David in
> another class.

Participant 5-Trevon. Trevon lives with his mom and two 24-year-old twin brothers. His mom is a manager at local restaurant and both his brothers are enrolled at an technical college in Denmark, South Carolina. Trevon describes himself as "tall, not really smart, and funny." Trevon is the tallest student in the fifth grade with long dreads that reach his shoulder. This school year is Trevon's second time in the fifth grade after transferring to Carolina Elementary in the last few months of the last school term. Several of the teachers that expressed concerns or problems with Trevon on last school term still teach him again this school term.

Trevon was described by his math teacher as a "surprise student" because "you never know what Trevon you will get. Some days you get the Trevon who just sits and does nothing all day and keeps to himself or Trevon the terror that's bothering everyone." Trevon has received seven office referrals within the first quarter of school because of his behavior and has been referred to the school's intervention team because he failed all of his major subjects for the first quarter. His was referred to the office because of "excessive talking," "disrupting class," "sleeping in class," "use of inappropriate language," "pants sagging," and "defiant to authority". His science teacher commented that:

> If Trevon doesn't take school and his life more seriously he will find himself in the fifth grade for a third year and that's no laughing matter. His mom does all she can to support him and the twins so its not like he don't know how to act. For some reason it's almost like he likes playing dumb. He thinks it funny! I told him last year he headed to the prison yard or McDonalds if he don't shape up. Especially now cuz some of the students are now saying he may be involved with some kind of neighborhood gang. Child, now days who knows? When I was his age I was still playing with dolls.

Several behavior charts and referral forms in Trevon's file describes him as "immature, thuggish, defiant, and a class clown" but contrastingly, notes that "he is respectful", "very conversational", and "friendly and warm when he wants to be." Trevon is often sent to the 'In School Suspension room (ISS room)' by several of his teachers whenever he misbehaves in class or comes to class unprepared. Three of Trevon's four major subject teachers even reported that they have sent him to the ISS room if they anticipate if he will come in the class and be disruptive or if they know they are having a observation by an administrator that day. His social studies teacher stated:

> I'm up to my wits with him. I'm serious! I can't take it no more. He
>
> talks non stop, cracks jokes, doesn't do work, or up out his seat.
>
> He's so focused at being either the class clown or bopping around
>
> like a thug. He messes up the class vibe. I almost lost my mind
>
> when I found out that boy was coming back here for another year.
>
> I'm done with Trevon for the year. Some days I can look at him in
>
> the hallway before he walks in and I can see he is about to be off the
>
> chain in my classroom. I don't even deal with him anymore, I just
>
> send him to ISS with some work to do to keep my sanity.

This school year, Trevon's mom decided to allow him to take a low dosage medication for Attention Deficit Hyperactive Disorder after several school officials and medical practitioner suggested it. His mom shared that:

> I really don't know what is going on with that boy. Before he got to
>
> the fifth grade he would get mostly A's & B's and the occasional C
>
> in math or something. He ain't really even get in trouble like this
>
> before either. I can remember maybe going up to the school maybe
>
> two times from kindergarten to the fourth grade for him talking and
>
> pushing another student. Now in 5th grade, we having all these
>
> problems with his behavior and grades. I just don't understand! I
>
> talk to Trevon all the time and tell him that you can't do nothing in
>
> life without an education. I never had this problem with my two

older sons, and they both in college now! I don't know what else to do. We will see if this medicine I just put him on will help. I work all kinds of hours and I just don't have the time to keep running back and forth up to this school. But I do know that I refuse to raise another Black boy to get wrapped up in the system or will either lay up and be a bomb when he grow up.

Trevon mentioned in his autobiography that he feels as though he is stupid and very frustrated about school. He says prefers to not have to come to school but does comes because his mother tells him often that he cannot do anything in life without an education. He said, "I guess that's why I try to keep coming so I can go to college and take care of my family one day." Trevon stated that he either wants to be a stand up comic like Kevin Hart when he grows up or go to college like his brothers to be an auto or computer technician.

Chapter Five:

Detrimental School Practices

Excessive use of worksheets and packets for busy work. One particular topic participants passionately exclaimed their abhorrence for in every interview was teachers' excessive use of worksheets (or packets of worksheets) during class time. David said he normally does packets in his classroom after every lesson. David explained, "It be a lot of them and it be stuff on them that you never been taught before how to do. They be real boring." When I asked Quincy if he learns things at school everyday he responded "no." Quincy said the days at school when he is not learning he is "reading, doing work, . . .like them packets", work he feels is "stuff to keep you quiet and busy." When I asked Hakeem what made school boring to him he said, "having to sit all day in the cold and. . .having to do a bunch of worksheets and reading." In fact, Hakeem's describes one of his four major classes as fun because, "we don't have to do a bunch of worksheets in there." Hakeem says, "not having to do worksheets" is what makes him happy in his classroom.

Similarly, when I asked Trevon if he would attend school if he did not have to he replied, "No I hate school (laughs)! It's boring. You sit all day and do packets and projects all day. You can't never have fun or can talk." All the participants, except Samuel, mentioned completing worksheets as one of the things that make them either bored or sad in class during their second interview. Trevon stated, "Things that make me sad is like when teachers be like do this worksheet and don't explain how to do it."

Later on during my focus group I asked the participants to name something teachers did in their classrooms that they did not like. Samuel answered, "When the teacher hand you a bunch of packets of worksheets to do and she sit back in her chair just chilling." Quincy

33

concurred with Samuel's statement and replied, "Ooo yea I hate that!" Trevon concluded the discussion by saying, "I don't even do 'em. When they pass out a bunch I just look at 'em."

Some of the participants resisted doing worksheets by either procrastination or by completely doing something else. David recalled a time when, "Mrs. Hearn came by my desk and snatched my pencil out my hand and grabbed my arm after I was drawing on my arm cuz I wasn't doing my worksheet. She walked …me down to the office and said I was refusing to do my work." Quincy claims, "sometimes we have so much stuff [worksheets] to do my hands be hurting from all the writing so . . .I just stop doing it." When I asked Quincy what happens when he refuses to continue doing the worksheets he replied, " I will probably get sent out or [the teacher will] say I'm refusing to do the work. I don't I just don't like my hand hurting."

During the focus group interview I asked Hakeem what reasons does he think students either disliked or wish they did not have to come back to school anymore. He answered:

> Peep this, like school real boring to them. Like nothing really
> interest them at school and they feel like school is a bunch of busy
> work and they don't do good at sitting and working by themselves in
> the quiet all day. Some people do better at like the alternative school.
> Quaz [and] them got sent there from the middle school and they like
> it better cuz they don't do things like a regular school. Some boys
> be trying to get enough write-ups so they can get sent there too.

Interpretation

It seemed to me the participants tended to get in trouble more frequently during their designated work time or when it appeared they felt as though their class work was mechanized, dull, "busy work." The participants usually resisted this monotonous work by intentionally slowing their pace by talking to others, procrastinating, drawing on their desk, or blatant refusal to work. As Ferguson (2001) noted, under tedious, routinized conditions of work and learning, activities that risk trouble, even trouble itself, function to spice up the school day and make time go by faster through creative attempts to make things happen and disrupt the routine.

Oakes (2005) further suggested the overuse of worksheets and drill curriculum is a way low-income and minority kids are schooled to take their place in the bottom rungs of the class structure. Oakes found that learning in low track and remedial classes are exposed to severely restricted knowledge base, requiring the most rudimentary learning process, rather than hands-on interactive learning experience that Gifted and Talented (GATE) students are exposed to. Based upon the participants' stories, I believe educators must be reflective of classroom practices that becomes mechanized, busy work for students. While educators may think packets/worksheets are good drill activities and helpful mechanisms to keep students quiet and busy, worksheets can be deleterious to the very desire to learn. As Hakeem mentioned, if students feel as though school is all a bunch of busy work to the point they prefer to be at an alternative school, worksheets and packets are perhaps one of the most dangerous activities to require of students.

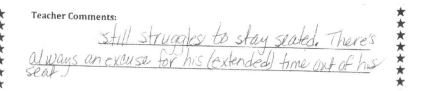

Figure 3.1. *Samuel's behavior chart regarding his movement in the classroom.*

Control of body movement. The participants all deeply valued the ability to move about their classroom and make decisions on how they controlled their body movements throughout the school; yet all the participants articulated their classrooms had specific rules and expectations that controlled students' body movements. Hakeem says the most boring part about school to him is "having to sit all day. . .and not being able to move until recess." Samuel exclaims, "me and other boys in my class normally gets in trouble for being up out of our seat because we at the pencil sharpener too long or just walking around for no reason." Samuel feels he gets bored in class when students have to sit in their "desk for the whole time." Samuel also contributes the ability to move about in the class as something that potentially could help him stay awake in class. Samuel explained:

> Recess be the time that I get to stretch my bones cuz when we get in
> the classroom we can't move and the teachers act like they want you
> to be a robot and don't ever move. And then the teachers be asking
> you why you stretching and I be saying, cuz my bones hurt so much
> from sitting that long.

Quincy feels as though teachers' expectations for body movement are "rules that don't really have a point." Quincy pointed out, "you cant move, . . . you got to stand in the third tile in the hall and, you gotta walk with your hands behind your back." During the focus group, Quincy reiterated his disdain by saying, "I don't like them rules that tell you you got to walk a certain way or sit a certain way in the desk. Like they try to tell you everything now. . .like they gon tell you how to sneeze soon." When I asked him what does he do when he has to sit for an extended period of time he replied, "I get bored and start to do stuff like draw or sleep." Quincy further exclaims:

That's why I can't really stand school. . .cuz like you come here and get in trouble for everything and you always getting fussed at. I get so tired of that. Like fussing all the time about everything. Like you get in trouble for. . .moving around too much, like anything.

Teacher Comments:

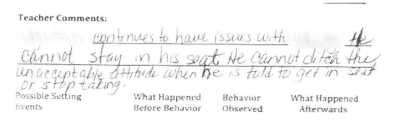

continues to have issues with
Cannot stay in his seat. He cannot ditch the
unacceptable attitude when he is told to get in seat
or stop taking.

| Possible Setting Events | What Happened Before Behavior | Behavior Observed | What Happened Afterwards |

Figure 3.2. Quincy's behavior chart regarding his constant movement within the classroom.

When I asked Hakeem what school or classroom rules bothers him the most he answered, "Students can't move around in Ms. Zorn's classroom without getting in trouble." Hakeem feels being "able to move around is fun cuz sitting in the desk all day is boring and it makes you sleepy." David shared with me, among other reasons, not being allowed to move around in his classroom was why his homeroom teacher, Mrs. Hearn, was his least favorite teacher. According to David:

> She don't let me do nothing. . .I can't move in her class. Chloe
> comes by my desk to get my work to turn in or somebody has to get
> things for me cuz she say I waste too much time being up
> daydreaming. So I have to stay in my seat the whole time.

David also mentioned his best day of school happened when Mrs. Lolly gave him four happy faces. David explained, "I came to school and didn't say nothing to nobody and didn't move. At the end of the day I had got four happy faces and some candy."

Some of the participants often spoke favorably of teachers that allowed movement within their classroom. Trevon says Mrs. Anders class is fun because "we can work under the table and on the floor if you want." One of the best parts about school to Samuel was when he was in the fourth grade class because "you could work on the floor and talk." Samuel says, "being able to work with people and move around and talk" in the classroom as one of the things that makes him happy. Hakeem believes being able to move about in the classroom, "help[s] me concentrate and stay focused like when I'm able to sit on the floor and stuff."

Interpretation

Normally, teachers at Carolina Elementary control the movements of children's bodies in their classrooms, leaving students unable to make decisions about how to regulate their body movement during the school day. Moving too quickly, or too slowly, or any movement at all can serve as a catalyst for a discipline referral as in the case of Quincy. Moreover, in the classroom, teachers demand children's bodies be arranged in certain positions before work can begin: sit up straight, both feet on the floor, hands off of the desk, eyes in front toward teacher, or down on the desk. Bodies must be properly arranged both individually and as a group before they can erupt from the classroom to play (Ferguson, 2001). Perhaps worst of all, students are suspended from school because of their inability to sit still in the classroom causing them to miss valuable class time.

All of the participants found having to sit all day in the desk as unfavorable. I argue that having to sit all day in a desk may even be detrimental to their specific learning style, as evidenced by Samuel's comments that, "sitting in the desk all day is boring and it makes you sleepy." Indeed, the participants valued the ability to move around the classroom and choose where they will sit to do their classwork. Trevon's comment corroborated their value of movement when he explained Mrs. Anders class was fun because, "we can work under the table and on the floor if you want."

Gurian (2007) noted, "The image of a schoolchild as someone sitting and reading has become the poster image for education, especially in the last fifty years. This is not a bad image-but it is an incomplete match with the way the minds of many of our boys work" (p. 123). Whitmire even argued:

> If a boy concludes he has great thoughts but knows he has trouble
> sitting still, he'll be okay. But if he concludes he can't have great
> thoughts because he can't sit still-that's another boy lost in the
> system who will never absorb all the skills schools should be passing
> along (Whitmire, 2011, p. 52).

I believe the intense surveillance of the participants' bodies are also because of other factors such as race and social class. Kaba (2010) asserts the emphasis on the orderly movement of students and their obedience to strict codes of conduct is also important both to schools' operational functioning and to their societal functions. Critical scholars such as Foucault (1977) and Bowles & Gintis (1976) have argued that strict disciplinary regimens in working class schools help to promote smooth and voluntary transitions into an industrial workplace that tightly regulates and subordinates laborers.

Recent empirical research by Nance (2013) indicated schools serving higher proportions of minority and low-income students are more likely to implement harsh, intense security conditions than other schools such as heavy restrictions on movement, having law enforcement present on campus, conducting random sweeps for contraband, and installing security cameras. The U.S. Department of Education (2012) even noted schools that rely on intense surveillance methods often have poor school climates that are detrimental to student learning and positive student growth, meaning; poor students and students of color often do not enjoy the same educational experiences that other students do. Furthermore, the use of intense surveillance methods is a component of a larger, more complex problem called the school-to-prison pipeline that disproportionately affects Black males than any other student demographic in our nation (Nance, 2013).

 Silence throughout the day. As Trevon eloquently stated in our first interview, "Its not about like just talking, like free time talking, but sometimes if you talk with a partner they can help you understand it. . .when I had worked with Jasmine I had understood it better." Like Trevon, each of the other participants mentioned their desire to be able to talk and collaborate with their peers more often than just at recess time. The participants echoed their disdain for the school-wide practice of having to be silent for most of the day. Quincy mentioned having to go to Ms. Colleton class is one of the worst parts about school because he feels, "She [is] aggravating. She always telling you what to do. . .You can't never talk in her class or move." Contrastingly, Quincy stated Mr. Reeve's class is one of the best parts about school because, "you can work in groups and work on the floor and talk."

 In his interview, David shared, "we normally have to be silent all day." When I asked him does he ever have time to talk during the day he replied:

> Yea at recess but I don't have them a lot. I normally have
> structured recess. . . [because] I probably start saying something to
> somebody at my table. Like we sit at tables of six so it's kind of
> hard to sit there the whole time and not say anything to anyone.

When I asked Samuel to describe his classroom for me he began by saying, "Umm it's a little bit crazy cuz my class love to talk. I'm one of the talkers that always gets in trouble." Hakeem expressed his value of being able to talk to his peers in class by

40

mentioning his homeroom teacher was "real nice" because "we can move around and talk in there."

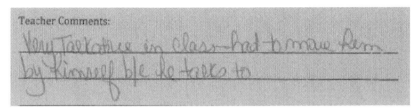

Figure 3.3. *Participant's behavior chart regarding his excessive talking.*

Interpretation

Throughout the school, signs are plastered on the walls of classrooms, in the hallway, and all about, bolstering the school's expectation and policy of students remaining silent during the school day. The students are expected to be silent in the hall, in the classroom (unless called upon), during lunch, and in the office. Young adolescents, particularly those in middle school or upper elementary students, begin to experience many physical, social, and emotional changes (Lorain, 2004). As MacWilliams (2000) asserts:

> A child's social development progresses along a continuum, from
> an egocentric world (the world revolves around him or her) to a
> world in which the child begins to work and play with other
> children to a world in which the child integrates his or her work and
> play with that of other children the same age. By early
> adolescence, the child's need for social interaction and being a part
> of the group is very strong . . . Factors such as a strong need to
> belong to a group and form friendships and creating an identity for
> themselves within and among a group are among several factors
> that drive the social behavior of young adolescents (para. 3).

41

Thus, early adolescence is a time students can readily be seen throughout Carolina Elementary whispering or passing notes during class time or talking with someone as they head to the pencil sharpener. Through talking and socializing, as Lorain (2000) noted, young adolescents project the human developmental stage they are in. As the participants expressed in this study who are either entering or in the adolescence stage, they have a strong desire to be able to talk and collaborate with their peers more often during the school day. The desire to talk is not only a natural facet of the participants' human development, but also appears to better suit their learning preferences. This notion is corroborated by David's comments during the focus group such as, "I can learn stuff from like my neighbor sometimes better than when the teachers explain it." When teachers and school leaders consider students' desire and social behavior of talking as a normal part of human development, they can plan school policies and classroom activities that are more suited for students' social development.

As Roger & Johnson (2014) asserts:

How students perceive each other and interact with one another
is a neglected aspect of instruction. Much training time is
devoted to helping teachers arrange appropriate interactions
between students and materials (i.e., textbooks, curriculum
programs) and some time is spent on how teachers should
interact with students, but how students should interact with one
another is relatively ignored. It should not be. How teachers
structure student-student interaction patterns has a lot to say
about how well students learn, how they feel about school and

42

the teacher, how they feel about each other, and how much self-esteem they have (para. 1).

Habitual conflict with substitute teachers. Trevon exclaimed, "If I know we gon have a sub, I try to stay home cuz I know if I come to school I'm definitely getting wrote up that day. Even if I act like Jalen (the school's character student representative) its still gon happen." This routine conflict between substitute teachers and the participants soon became a dominant pattern that emerged to me throughout the participant interviews. This topic was first mentioned by Hakeem when he answered, "stop making the class just sit for hours," after I asked him what can teachers do to help you learn better. I asked him what he meant by the class just sitting and Hakeem explained, "Like doing work for the entire class time or having to be quiet and just sit there the whole period. This happens a lot when we have subs." Hakeem noted, "everytime we have one [a substitute teacher] I get in trouble," a fact he believes is because:

> Sometimes the teacher will leave a note and tell them who the bad
>
> students are and to send us out if we do anything or they will say
>
> like they know who the bad students are just by looking at us.

After hearing many of the participants identify substitute teachers as persons they have routine conflict with in school, I decided to ask the participants why they felt like it was routine to get in trouble with substitutes during the focus group. David told me:

> You try to help them [substitute teachers] and that's when they get
>
> mad and say they gon write you up for helping them. I remember
>
> when Mrs. Singletary was about to let a bunch of students leave the
>
> class and I told her we not supposed to do that. That's when she
>
> sent me out for being disrespectful.

Quincy shared, "I don't even be doing nothing! Them subs come up in there and the first thing they say is 'Alright now boy the first thing you do today ima send you out!'"

Trevon echoed his sentiments regarding substitute teachers by stating:

> Every time we have a sub I get all these write ups. I go weeks
> without one and then when a sub come, I always get in trouble. I
> get in trouble with them for having my head down, talking, or
> anything. . . Like they come and just sit there. And for like eight
> hours they want us to sit down, don't move, don't talk, and do
> worksheets the entire day. That's why people get in trouble.

I asked Trevon if he feels like he gets in trouble easier with substitutes versus his regular teachers and he responded:

> Kinda. . .Like the subs will be like I remember you from last time
> so Ima be watching you, so they come in waiting for anything you
> do to send you out. Like days we have subs I just be like I should
> have stayed home.

Also during the focus group Samuel shared he believes the reason he gets in trouble with substitute teachers is because:

> They walk in and judge you and be like these the bad boys, so they
> be trying to be extra tough on you to prove they can be a good sub.
> . .They just abuse they power and just write people up for any little
> thing.

Quincy believes the routine conflict with substitutes is because, "Subs don't know you and so they gon blame stuff on you quicker than your regular teacher will sometimes too." Trevon added, "everybody get wrote up when we have subs cuz they don't know what they doing and they like to talk to the class any kind of way." David concurred with the other participants and shared, "But then now, some teachers will leave a list of bad kids for them to look out for, that's why they have certain kids they will start messing with."

Interpretation

U.S. teachers take off an average of 9.4 days each or 5% of regular school days during a typical 180-day school year, and substitute teachers are called to fill in for absent teachers (U.S. Dept. of Education, 2010). This means the average public school student has substitute teachers for more than six months of his or her school career. As Glatfelter (2006) suggested, "Substitute teachers are charged with creating the "best approximation of the teaching that would have taken place had the regular teacher been present" (p. 18). Thus, in the most optimal circumstances, substitute teachers help alleviate the disruptive impact on student learning caused by the absence of their regular teacher. Most substitute teachers usually have one-day, or fairly short-term assignments and educational backgrounds ranging from a highschool diploma to the bachelors level (Damle, 2009). According to the sparse research and other documented evidence, while substitute teachers are able to keep students busy with work, they accomplish very little by way of serious instruction and student learning (p.1).

As in the case of the participants, it is obvious there are some severe problems between students and substitute teachers that soon need to be addressed. This is apparent from school administrators that indicate the number of office referrals increase when substitute teachers are employed for the day and also from several of the participants' comments. As Hakeem shared, when substitutes are present students are either kept busy with work to fill the time or expected to sit quietly for the class duration. Consequently, this leaves two school practices the participants have articulated that makes them angry, bored or sad in the classroom--being kept busy with work and the expectation to sit quietly for the entire class duration. I believe this is why every participant has at least one office referral on file for the current academic year from a substitute teacher.

Teachers also appear to add "fuel to the fire" by giving their substitute teachers a list of bad students to be on the look out for. This can certainly exacerbate substitute teachers' perceptions and preconceived notions about students based upon immediate factors such as race, clothing, dialect, and etc. they carry into the classrooms with them. This notion is corroborated by comments like Samuel's when he said, "they walk in and judge you and be like these the bad boys so they be trying to be extra tough on you to prove they can be a good sub."

Lack of incorporation of different modalities/intelligences of learning in classroom activities. Throughout my data collection, Samuel frequently mentioned his desire to engage in classroom activities that employed other modes of learning than the predominant visual and auditory modalities and the verbal and linguistic intelligences. Samuel shared how much he enjoyed Mr. Simuel's class in the fourth grade, his first male teacher. Samuel exclaimed:

> He was great! I learned a lot in his class. His class was real fun, we would make stuff, go on field trips, some of his Frat brothers would come to the school and show us steps. . .he was Black too. . .he would rap for us and talk about rappers and things we liked. That was the best teacher of my life. I was smart in his class.

When I asked Samuel why he felt smart in Mr. Simuel's class he said, "Cuz that was the only year I almost made A/B honor roll. Like for our science project he let me sing a song about the different cloud types instead of doing a test." Later on during the focus group Samuel shared he believes some students begin to dislike school because:

> Like you can't really do the stuff you really like doing or good very
>
> often. Like for me, I like music but I only come to music once a
>
> week. But see like I use music all the time cuz sometimes I be
>
> thinking about like the music notes in like math to help me and
>
> stuff.

 Hakeem shared his enjoyment of being allowed to use his interests and creativity in the classroom more often during our first interview as well. Hakeem told me he would like to "have all the Brothers' Keepers in the same class" because they were all "Black and boys," something that makes him more comfortable. He said:

> We all [the boys in the Brothers' Keeper Program] like the same
>
> type of music and sports and stuff and we do those things in. . .our
>
> work. Like. . .we wrote about what would we do if we could be the
>
> host of 106th and Park last week during our journal time or we
>
> could do jumping jacks during multiplication tournament. Oh and
>
> we can make a rap song as a project for the Reconstruction era we
>
> learned about.

Quincy also shared his wish to make class "more fun" by "not reading so much but like….building and making stuff and doing more projects in the science lab."

Interpretation

 Samuel, Quincy, and Hakeem's stories illustrated that students learn in a variety of ways and have their own problem-solving capabilities. In the 20th century, two educational theories, learning modalities theory and multiple intelligences theory, were put forward in an attempt to interpret human differences and to design educational models around these differences. Silver, Strong, & Perini (1997) noted learning modalities theory emphasizes the sensory channels or pathways in which individuals give, receive, and store information. The theory of multiple intelligences theory highlights the various capacities to solve problems or fashion products that are valued in one or more cultural setting.

Thus, as Samuel and Hakeem both expressed their adoration for being able to create songs and raps using content they learned for formal assessments, these students are actually expressing what Gardner (1993) posits as their preference to use their musical intelligence. Musical intelligence, one of the eight intelligences that Gardener suggested, uses students' imaginative and expressive abilities to interpret ideas and concepts. Creating songs and raps using course content, is a unique classroom activity that utilizes the musical intelligence. This is rather unique type of assessment compared to the visual and mathematical intelligences, which are the predominant intelligences used in classrooms (Gardner, 1993).

Utilizing a variety of learning modalities in the classroom is important too. Hakeem noted he is able to do jumping jacks while learning multiplication facts, this of course, is utilizing one the four learning modalities, kinesthetic. This sensory way of learning using movement has several implications within the classroom. While it helps students that learn best while moving, it also promotes physical movement and helps engage students throughout the lesson. Thus, when teachers utilize various modes of teaching and classroom activities to accommodate the different modalities and intelligences, student engagement and learning can significantly be maximized.

Chapter Six:

Negative Teacher Interactions

Feeling unprepared to be academically successful. In different ways, all of the participants expressed they felt unprepared to be academically successful in their classrooms. When I asked Samuel what classes is he most bored in he replied, "Probably science and math cuz. . .it ain't never really taught how to do it in a way you can understand. You just do work and get a bunch of grades but you don't know what you're doing." When I asked Samuel why he does not ask for help he explained, "if I don't understand something. . .I sit there and try to figure it out but by then I normally get bored and start doing something else." He further noted, "sometimes in Mrs. Forrest class I don't ask her nothing cuz I don't too much like her. . . [because] you just don't feel like getting told you should have been paying attention before they help you."

When I asked Trevon what class does he get the most bored in he answered:

Science and social studies cuz all they do is talk and pass out work.

They don't really even explain how to do it really. They just be

reading out the book. Especially Ms. Buyer. She always reading

stuff out the book.

Quincy noted his old school was aggravating because:

She [his math teacher] didn't even teach you, cuz like the teachers

there don't really help you. She. . .would give you a worksheet and

don't tell you how to do it. And then she'll. . .call my name cuz I

used to sit there and draw on the desk or something cuz I didn't

know how to do it.

David shared his favorite teachers was Ms. Willette and Mrs. Love because, "Mrs. Willette explain math in a way I can understand and gives me things when I do good things. And Mrs. Love helps me out extra and won't leave my desk until I understand it." David feels other teachers does not teach him in a way he can understand because, "if they don't really like you they not gon help you as much. . .they just gon kinda let you be on your own." When I asked David why he believes he gets bad grades he said:

> I don't know. I try to do the work I know how to do. Sometimes I
> don't really understand the stuff so I don't do it. . .my mommy or
> daddy help me with it when I go home but the way they show me
> don't be the way we do it in class.

When I asked David what could his teachers do to teach him better he said, "not go on in the lesson until everyone got it. Like once the smart kids in class got it we always move on before. . .us slow kids get it." David said he knows he is one of the "slow kids" because, "the smart kids are the ones that get picked on for everything and they finish they work fast. They the ones the teacher like." Hakeem expressed similar sentiments by explaining Mrs. Bean was his least favorite teacher because, "she don't help you. If you don't understand something you will just fail." Hakeem says he wants his teachers to know, "They need to help me. . .like stop telling me to figure it out on my own and come to my desk and help me instead of brushing me off."

Interpretation

The participants all mentioned many reasons why they each felt as though they were unprepared to be academically successful in the classroom. The three salient reasons participants shared is either: a) teachers passed out work and did not explain how to complete the assignment, b) poor teacher-student relationship influenced how much the teacher assisted them academically, or c) the teacher's attention were more focused on the "smart kids" grasping the lesson rather than the "slow kids."

Arnold (2001) asserts:

Busy work allows students to work independently, to test their own knowledge and skills, and to practice using new skills learned in the educational setting. It can consist of various types of schoolwork assigned by a teacher to keep students occupied with activities involving learning and cognition while the teacher focuses upon another group of students. . .The perceived results of the work by students is significant: when students feel that they've succeeded in accomplishing a functional task, it's congruent with learning and the attainment of new skills.

While busy work keeps the students occupied and rehearses skills students have already learned, busy work is rarely employed by teachers to teach a new concept. Thus, when students are unable to complete assignments they regard as busy work, there lies a significant problem; students should learn the skill the worksheet is intended to drill and assess before it is passed out. If a student cannot complete or even begin the practice assignment the teacher assigns, the student has not truly learned the content. At this moment teachers should reteach or scaffold learning for the student. However, in the case of the participants, it appears to me their class assignments are simply used to occupy time.

Participants like David and Quincy also expressed their belief that their ability to succeed in the classroom is connected with their relationship with the teacher. David and Quincy beliefs are supported within educational literature. Research indicates children who experience a negative teacher-student relationship in elementary school often have lower academic achievement throughout their schooling tenure (Buyse, Verschueren, Verachtert, & Van Damme, 2009). Baker (2006) asserts teacher relationship quality is especially important for students with behavior difficulties or learning problems. Students that have close relationships with their teachers show significant advantages compared to similar classmates without such relationships (Baker, 2006). Klem & Connel (2004) noted when students both perceive their teachers as supportive and feel as though they are participants in a classroom where expectations are appropriate, fair, and clearly communicated, students are likely to have better school attendance rates and higher scores on assessments. School assessments and attendance rates are also predictors of high school graduation rates and college enrollment.

Finally, students that feel as though the "smart kids" dictate their classroom's learning pace represents a old and complex problem in American schools. Petrilli (2011) asserts the greatest challenge facing America's schools today isn't the budget crisis, or standardized testing, or "teacher quality," it's the enormous variation in the academic level of students coming into any given classroom. Thus, the arguable compromise educators must make is to choose between controversial ability grouping or often, unreasonable differentiated instructional plans. Unfortunately, while these compromises are still being debated, participants like David are being left behind in the classroom.

Intentional student embarrassment. One salient pattern that was consistently expressed by each participant was their enmity for being embarrassed by the teachers in front of their peers and others. Trevon says he dislikes going to class because, "them teachers like to shine on you. . .ya know, they like to blast you in front of everyone or try to embarrass you cuz they can." Hakeem shared his similar experience by saying one of the worst parts about school is, "Mrs. Peeler or Mrs. Bean. . .will try to embarrass you in front of everyone. That be pissing me off." Hakeem added:

> They tell everyone your bad grades if you got them or your
> business. Like every bad thing you ever did in your life, and do it
> in the hallway or [in front of] the whole class so everyone can hear.
> My daddy say they be trying to set me up to make me mad enough
> to say something back so they will have a lot of witnesses.

When I asked Samuel what made him angry in his classroom he answered:

When teachers telling people that I got kept back in front of everyone. That's just embarrassing you know. You don't be wanting people to know that. You just want this new year to be a new chance and not think about last year.

David also expressed this shared perspective when he stated his worst day of school was when:

> I was. . .in the cafeteria and I was talking to Randy, and Mrs. Hearn
> told me to stand up. She was yelling telling everyone that that's
> why I had bad grades, cuz I don't listen. She said out loud that I
> need to go home and tell my daddy that that's reason why I make
> bad grades, and need to stop lying saying she picking on me. . .[I
> felt] sad and mad cuz she [told] everyone in there that I make bad
> grades.

David expressed Mrs. Hearn was his least favorite teacher because she routinely calls his name to answer questions in class whenever he does not complete his homework. He feels Mrs. Hearn does this to, "embarrass me for not doing my work and show I don't know nothing. . .one time I rolled my eyes at her when she called my name six times." David explained, "I didn't get mad with her until she said aloud that I was gonna get kept back cuz I don't never do my homework."

Quincy believes mean teachers like to push his buttons by yelling at him in front of his friends with the intent of trying to embarrass him. Quincy expressed:

> Last year, Ms. Gosling got up in my face saying stuff about me in
> front of everyone in front of everyone and then when my momma
> got here, she gon act like she don't be doing that stuff. She like to
> lie. I hated her.

Interpretation

Looking at the teacher-student interactions from the participants' perspectives, I believe certain teachers intentionally embarrass them in front of their peers. The intended outcome for this embarrassment is not explicitly known, however, I postulate this is done because of various reasons such as an class management technique of "making an example" out of the participant. This action is likely an attempt to publicly discredit the integrity of the participant, or an product of the teacher's disdain or frustration with him.

According to Covington (1992), students engage in some behaviors considered detrimental to learning, such as avoiding seeking help in order to protect their self-worth. Situations in which students are likely to be judged negatively or embarrassed by adults or peers will often result in students' avoidance of these situations or dislike of the teacher exhibiting the behavior (Covington, 1992). Thus, students may avoid asking questions or participating if they feel doing so would demonstrate a lack of knowledge or ability. This research is corroborated by David's story when he explained he does not respond to the many times Mrs. Hearn calls on him to answer questions in class to demonstrate to his peers he did not complete his homework or know the content.

When a teacher intentionally embarrasses a student daily, Kelmon (2014) asserts this behavior becomes an act of bullying of a teacher towards a student. Alward (2006) noted 2% of children are bullied by a teacher sometime in their elementary or middle school years. There is a glaring absence of research and statistics on the effects of intentional student embarrassment and adult school bullies. Alward (2006) however suggested, teacher bullying can take form whenever a teacher takes a dislike to certain students in their class and humiliates or degrades the student in front of his peers, or decides to consistently reprimand a student in public. The effects of ongoing intentional embarrassment, or teacher bullying, towards students can have tremendous impact on students' engagement and value of school and their relationship with their teacher (Kelmon, 2014). This makes this teacher interaction incredibly dangerous, particularly for African American males who represents the largest demographic of students labeled as "at-risk" at Carolina Elementary.

Aggressive student-teacher interaction. Many of the participants were extremely bothered whenever they felt as though a teacher interacted with them aggressively through physical and verbal contact. I asked Quincy what he thought would be some reasons why some students either disliked school or wished they did not have to come back anymore. Quincy responded, "Like the teachers will point they finger in your face and walk up on you like they about to whip you or something. Quincy expressed, "Don't treat students bad…don't be pulling on them to get in line or getting in they face yelling. They [teachers] wouldn't want it done to them. Let one of us do it to them. They would kick us out so fast."

Figure 6.1 *A participant's Think Sheet response for why he decided to knock over his books on his desk during class.*

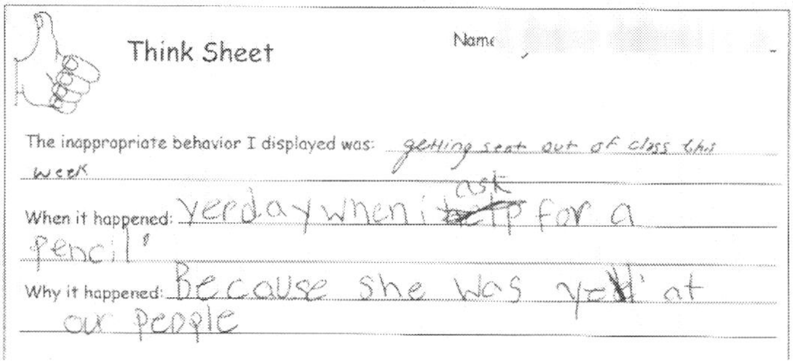
Think Sheet

Name

The inappropriate behavior I displayed was: getting seat out of class this week

When it happened: yerday when i ask for a pencil

Why it happened: Because she was yell' at our people

When I asked David has he ever gotten in trouble with one of his current teachers David responded, "I get in trouble everyday!" He explained:

> You can not do anything and still get in trouble….like umm, Mrs. Hearn came by my desk and snatched my pencil out my hand and grabbed my arm after I was drawing on my arm cuz I wasn't doing my worksheet. She walked…me down to the office and said I was refusing to do my work, but I told them I wasn't but she said I was. I just don't like when she snatches things and be jerking on me. She makes me hate school sometimes.

When I asked Hakeem the same question he told me:

> Yea today. Mrs. Bean yelling in my face in the hallway and she put her finger in my face. Then she gon grab my arm and kinda

like push me in the back of line. I called her a bitch underneath my

breath. She asked me what I said but I aint say never say nothing

back. I just ignored her.

Hakeem said he responded that way because he asked her if he could go to the bathroom and, "she talking bout no cuz I'm probably one of the ones that's been drawing graffiti on the stalls." Samuel said he felt like his second grade teacher did not like him because, "Ms. Kennedy would say I don't study or that I was being lazy. . .and shout in my face…I would get mad and shout at her and say I do work…and she would send me out." Samuel later shared "when teachers get in your face and be pointing and screaming at you," as one of the things which makes him angry in his classroom. According to Samuel:

They [teachers] come to the school with a bad attitude and want to

talk to us any kind of way and expect for us to just sit and take it.

Like if we get an attitude we get sent out, but if they do when we

asking a simple question, than it's ok. Sometimes, I just don't even

say nothing in class cuz I don't feel like dealing with em.

Interpretation

Montalvo, Mansfield, & Miller (2007) asserts certain teacher traits serve as strong indicators of students' like or dislike for school. Teacher interactions with students that can be deemed as aggressive, forceful, and even hostile at times, as in the case of the participants, are particular teacher traits that can construct a student's dislike for school. Research studies (Birch & Ladd, 1997; Klem & Connell, 2004; Montalvo et al., 2007) indicate teachers who experience close relationships with students reported their students were less likely to avoid school, appeared more self-directed, more supportive, and more engaged in learning. In addition, students attain better grades in classes taught by teachers they like (Montalvo et al., 2007). Thus, there is relationship between student-teacher interactions and student achievement.

The public education system continues to struggle to improve the substantial gap between the educational achievement between Whites and Black students in the U.S. Being such, students and teachers must mutually be cognizant of the immense responsibility they each share in ensuring optimal educational goals. However, teachers hold an immense degree of power over their students and are the professionals within the classroom. Though interactions such as yelling and intimidating physical actions (finger pointing, snatching items, tugging on articles of clothing, invading student's personal space) may be a teacher's way of ensuring students compliance in the classroom, managing the classroom through an atmosphere of fear will never quite establish a respectful classroom environment with positive student-teacher relationships.

Linsin (2012) noted most teachers who use methods like intimidation, do so in lieu of following their classroom management plan—which causes resentment and distrust between students and teachers and makes the teacher's ability to build rapport and influence virtually impossible. This is particularly true for my participants who all named teachers who used methods of intimidation towards them as their least favorite teacher. Ultimately, the participants' feelings about their teachers influenced the way they engaged and valued school. This is illustrated by comments by David and Samuel's where, "I just don't like when she snatches things and be jerking on me. She makes me hate school sometimes" and "Sometimes I just don't even say nothing in class cuz I don't feel like dealing with em," respectively.

Teachers' degrading comments. A rather unfortunate pattern that emerged from the data is the participants' sadness and anger towards the degrading comments their teachers

58

make towards them. Hakeem mentioned he gets angry when teachers speak to him "any kind of way. . .and not liking you." Hakeem later explained:

> My teacher done told me plenty of times I'm a thug, a wannabe
> gangsta, or gonna be on the corner. She said I got jail written on
> my forehead. She done even told the principal I was in a gang. But
> you ain't gotta believe the stuff they tell you though.

Quincy named three teachers as his least favorite teachers because of the "racist stuff" they have said to him. Quincy said they say things like, "I'm going to jail when I grow up or I will never graduate and be a thug." He shared:

> Like today, Mrs. Colleton gon say that I copied Desiree homework
> and that if I can't learn to do the right thing and tell the truth, Ima
> grow up in jail. And I said I ain't going to jail and she said I was
> talking back and told me to go sit in the hall.

Quincy later elaborated, "just because you stole something one time doesn't mean that you gonna be a thug or criminal when you grow up. It just means you made a mistake one time as a kid." When I asked Trevon to tell me how he thinks his teacher feels about him he answered:

> She probably think Ima grow up and be a drug head and be on the
> streets…she be like…if I don't grow up and do better in school,
> Ima be a drug dealer on the streets or dead or in jail.

Later on when I asked Trevon what was something he wished his teacher knew about him he said, "That I can make A's and B's and I ain't no thug."

The two participants (Samuel & David) who were labeled academically "at-risk" by Carolina Elementary, shared how non-criminalistic comments could also be degrading to students. Samuel expressed:

> Mr. Anderson I swear this gets on my nerves! Like if you ask a teacher a question cuz you didn't hear or understand and they say, you shoulda been paying attention the first time…I just don't like that. That's the worst thing about the teachers here. They do that a lot. Cuz sometimes you know, you just don't hear or understand something. That thing bother me, so I don't even ask questions sometimes cuz I don't wanna hear it.

In my second interview Samuel expressed he felt as though his second grade teacher Ms. Kennedy did not like him because, "Ms. Kennedy would say I don't study or that I was being lazy and not applying myself and I would get mad and shout at her and say I do work at em [multiplication time tables] and she would send me out." David expressed similar sentiments when he told me, "my teachers say I spoil everything. They don't like me so I don't ask no questions…Ms. Denver said I spoil things because I blurt out answers before others or tell others what we gon learn for that day." David also shared his teachers said he was a bad influence on the class because he likes to be a class clown and talk to others and get them in trouble. When I asked David would he prefer for teachers to not tell students when they act bad he responded by saying:

> Well kinda. You can tell them what they did wrong. But like when kids hear stuff like that, they get mad and then, what happens if they get in jail when they get older or do the bad things the teacher said they was gone do? That person gon be like, that's what my

teacher said about me when I was a kid so she help put me here. In
my other school the teachers tell you that so they can scare you
from doing it [getting in trouble].

Samuel concluded our discussion on this topic during the focus group by noting
if teachers:

Say it [degrading comments] so much you can start to believe it.
Like if teachers keep calling you lazy like mine used to, one day
you gon be like ain't no point in trying so hard cuz they just gon
say I'm lazy anyway.

Interpretation

It is very unfortunate the participants are subjected to these daily racial
microaggressions within the school. Racial microaggressions are "brief, everyday exchanges
that send denigrating messages to people of color because they belong to a racial group" (Sue,
Bucceri, et al., 2007, p.72). Nadal (2008b) noted whether intentional or not,
microaggressions may result in student's frustration, alienation, anger, and other emotions
that come from being belittled. Degrading comments such as calling students lazy, thugs,
prison inclined, or future drug dealers can even cause negative emotions that may eventually
result in mental problems including depression and anxiety (Nadal, 2008b). Other teacher
comments like what Samuel mentioned such as "you should have been paying attention,"
whenever he asks his teacher a question assumes the student is at fault for not knowing the
intended information and does not take into account the possibility that they student could
have either missed the information or does not understand it. In both cases, comments like
these can influence students to not participate in class and increase feelings their alienation
from school and their classroom.

61

Chapter Seven:

Acts of Marginalization Towards Black Male Students

Sagging Pants. There were several school practices that caused Black students, notably Black male students, to experience marginalization within Carolina Elementary. A unique topic that was mentioned throughout all of my interviews was all of the participants, with the exception of David, frequently mentioned getting in trouble or either having a problem with teachers' policing of sagging pants. Quincy expressed during the focus group, "Some teachers be treating sagging like you brought a bomb to school. They be yelling at you and be writing you up. They make too big of a deal about it." I asked Hakeem why he said some of the teachers are not good teachers at the school and he responded, "Cuz some of them like to treat you like a thug or something. They always be bothering me about my pants sagging."

Hakeem says his issue with the sagging pants is, "Everyday Mrs. Peeler say she gon take away my recess or write me up cuz my pants too low or baggy. She say school ain't the place to dress like I'm about to stand on the corner." However, Hakeem does not think his pants sag. Hakeem explained, "I get my pants from my big brother so they be real baggy. They be looking like I'm sagging. . .I don't think you should get in trouble just for the way you dress. It ain't like its bothering anybody." In fact, Hakeem says teachers reprimanding him constantly throughout the school day about sagging pants make him very angry.

Trevon recalled often being scolded by teachers for his pant's sagging too. When I asked Trevon how he feels about the pants rule he said, "they want you to dress like White boys do I guess cuz White boys don't sag." Trevon feels:

I don't think it's that big of a deal. Like at home it don't be no big

deal but at school you can get sent home for it or your recess taken.

But they don't be saying nothing about what anybody else be

wearing though.

Samuel admittedly reported there were:

A few times she told me to pull them up but not like Tyson & them.

She have to write them up or send them to the office cuz she have

to tell them all the time. All the Black boys in my class normally

get in trouble about that.

When I asked Samuel why he thinks Black boys in class normally gets in trouble

for the way they wear their clothes he explained:

I don't know. I figure White people don't really like it. A lot of

Black people do it but there some Black people that fuss about it

too. I think people just dress the way they want. My grandma

don't let me come out the house like that so it don't bother me too

much.

Teacher Discipline Referral Form

Student: _____ Referring Staff: _____

School: _____ Grade: _4_ Date: _9-16-14_ Time: _8:27am_

Location:
☐ Bathroom ☐ Cafeteria ☐ Courtyard ☑ Hallway ☐ Office ☐ Playground ☐ School Grounds
☐ Bus ☑ Classroom ☐ Gym ☐ Media Center ☐ Parking Lot ☑ School Activity

Incident Description:
Has to be told several times a day to pull up his pants. This has been on going since the first week of school.

Teacher Signature: _____

For Administrative Use Only

Incident Code:

Figure 7.1. *Teacher discipline referral form reprimanding one of my participants for sagging his pants.*

Interpretation

Perhaps the most interesting notion about the sagging pants disciplinary measure is the school nor the school district in which the participants attends has an official policy regarding students' sagging their pants. The school has an official policy on inappropriate student attire such as n restriction on skirts that are above the knee or wearing shirts with guns, profanity, drugs, or sex in it, however, there are no signs within the school that reminds students of the official student-attire policy. Contrastingly, several teacher-made signs are posted on classroom doors and walls regarding expectations about sagging pants, all depicting human characters of color. Students, almost exclusively Black boys, are readily referred to the office because of sagging pants and numerous student files contain teacher-made memos and comments regarding sagging pants. All except one of my participants have either been referred to the office or had their recess taken because of this hidden rule.

Figure 7.2. *A teacher-made sign posted on classroom door at Carolina Elementary.*

It appears certain ways and articles of dress have become identified by school officials as non-conformist, thuggish, gang-like and harbingers of dangerous anti-school expressions, including the no sagging pants ruling. The teacher-made signs regarding sagging pants alludes sagging as an specific issue among Black students only and subliminally tells all students within the school Black students' dress is to be closely monitored and policed. This is perhaps one of the most salient examples of how teachers use race and culture as a filter in the interpretive work of making judgments about the actions of their students, particularly African American males. The school-wide effort to infuse institutional discourses and practices upon these students thru the cultural inversion of clothing style may have appeared well intended, but instead, is a reproduction of Gramsci's (1992) hegemony and systems of cultural superiority. Hegemony, as Gramsci (1992) defines, occurs when the ruling class manipulates the lower classes by manipulating the culture of society with the beliefs, explanations, perceptions, and values so the ruling-class worldview is imposed and accepted as the cultural norm.

To the participants, their style of clothing seemed normal as illustrated by Trevon's comments that "at home it [sagging] don't be no big deal but at school you can get sent home for it or your recess taken." One of the more interesting notions about the policing of sagging pants within the school is that the participants' teachers that issued disciplinary sanctions because of their sagging pants were mostly Black women. In fact, all of the teacher made signs and posters posted about sagging pants throughout the school were all by Black female faculty. In an informal interview with one of those teachers she informed me:

> These boys don't know how they are setting themselves up for failure. When they go about this school looking like some drug boy you think these White women gon show them any more respect? Hell naw they ain't! I'm here to teach these kids not only bout they books but life skills too. You can't get a job going to an interview like that. People gon judge them just based off the way they look. Look at what happened to Trevon Martin! Our boys already struggling enough. They don't need to fuel the fire by dressing like the hoodlums they think we are anyway. I grew up poor 'round these same parts as these boys. But one thing is my parents valued how you looked and they valued education. And I know that some of these young parents don't instill that no more but I'm here to tell them pull em up anyway! They may not like me now but they will thank me later.

To me, the Black teachers appears to particularly advocate and enforce the no sagging policy as a way to help Black boys blend into the dominant school culture and learn how to survive in the real world. As Rios (2006) asserts, "While most of the adults in the community care about the youth they interact with, most are uncritical of how their epistemology shapes the way in which they treat and criminalize the youth they are attempting to support" (p.52). Rio's describes this "hypercriminalization" as the "youth control complex" which is defined as "a system in which schools, police, probation officers, families, community centers, the media, businesses, and other institutions systemically treat young people's everyday behaviors as criminal activity" (p. 50). These educators' rigorous policing on sagging pants are a prime example of this "youth control complex" in action. Rios noted:

Young people, who become pinballs within this youth control complex, experience what I refer to as hypercriminalization, the process by which an individual's everyday behaviors and styles become ubiquitously treated as deviant, risky, threatening or criminal, across social contexts. This hypercriminalization, in turn, has a profound impact on young people's perceptions, worldviews, and life outcomes. The youth control complex creates an overarching system of regulating the lives of marginalized young people, what I refer to as punitive social control. Hypercriminalization involves constant punishment. Punishment, in this study, is understood as the process by which individuals come to feel stigmatized, outcast, shamed, defeated, or hopeless as a result of negative interactions and sanctions imposed by

individuals who represent institutions of social control (2006, p.52).

Prohibition of "Ebonics" or "Black English." One interesting pattern that

surfaced only among the 5th grade participants Trevon, Samuel, and Hakeem is the practice of

participants being prohibited and reprimanded for using Black English or Ebonics within the

classroom, specifically the two ELA classes taught by two White, middle class, women.

Hakeem first mentioned in the second interview one of the things that makes him angry in

class is "getting your recess taken or sent out for stupid stuff like talking wrong." He

elaborated, "you can't say certain words in. . .class cuz they say it's wrong. Some big word

like [Ebonics]. . .if you keep using it you will get your recess taken."

Trevon echoed his frustration with this unofficial 5th grade policy by exclaiming, "I

hate stuff like in Ms. Zorn class you get sent out for the way you talk. Trevon described, "her

list she got on the wall got things that you can't say in her class or you will get clipped down.

. .like 'ain't', 'on-fleek', umm stuff like that." He also described Ms. Zorn's clip down

process is, "If you get clipped down on the chart you get. . .your recess taken or a phone call

home. Sometimes you can get wrote up if you get days after days of clip downs." Samuel,

though he never specifically mentioned getting in trouble for using Ebonics or Black English

in class, said, " [teachers] stopping me all the time while I talk to correct the way I speak"

makes him very angry. Later on during the focus group interview Samuel says the one thing

he really does not like about his classroom is that "you can't use certain words in class."

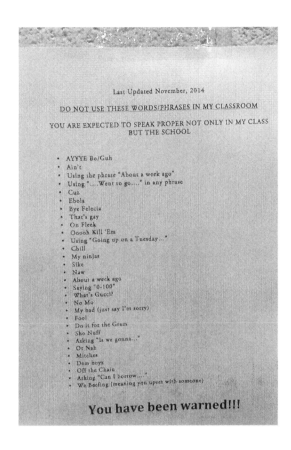

Figure 7.3. *A teacher's sign posted in her classroom regarding her policy on restricted language.*

<u>Interpretation</u>

The prohibition of Black English or Ebonics was a unique pattern that only occurred with the fifth grade participants. Personally, this pattern was particularly startling for me as it was one of the more blatant forms of hegemony that positioned Black students to believe their dialect and language is inferior to "Standard English." As Christensen (2009)

69

noted, educators have the power to determine whether students feel included or excluded in schools and classrooms. By bringing student's home language into the classroom, teachers validate students' culture and history as topics worthy of study. Contrastingly, when teachers denigrate student's culture by restricting students' use of language in the classroom, teachers inadvertently suggest something is wrong with the student and promotes cultural inferiority. For teachers to question rather students should be allowed to use or not use Ebonics, Delpit (1998) asserts:

> I can be neither for Ebonics or against Ebonics any more than I can be against air. It exists. It is the language spoken by many. . .African American children. It is the language they heard as their mothers nursed them. . . It is the language through which they first encountered love, nurturance, and joy (p.17).

Most teachers of African American children who have been the least well served by educational systems, believe their students' chances will be further impeded if they do not learn "Standard English" (Depit, 1998). This is probably true for the teachers of the participants, however; what may have been initialized with good intentions, now has taken the form of a classroom policy that criminalizes and oppresses speakers of Black English. These teachers are probably unaware the Linguistic Society of America (1997), the largest linguistic society in the world, affirmed and substantiated Black English as legitimate, rule-based, and systematic, spoken by approximately 80% of Black students. Boutte (2008) asserts perceptions of Black English or any other language have more to do with larger sociopolitical beliefs about the group speaking the language than the actual language itself. Thus, as a group, while African Americans continue to be marginalized in the United States, it is comprehensible why Black English is viewed as inferior "street language" compared to

"Standard English." Teachers should instead utilize "code switching" with their students and teach them the appropriate settings & mechanics to use King's English instead of totally denigrating students of color native tongue.

Assumption of deviancy without proof. The participants shared their experiences with, and resentment about, adults within the school building that readily assumed they are devious and guilty in all negative situations, even without evidence. These adults apparently assumed the participants were blameworthy either because the participants were found guilty of the action in the past or the participant had a lasting reputation throughout the school for being devious and troublesome. These assumptions tended to occur more often with participants that were deemed "at-risk" by the school for behavioral problems more so than participants labeled "at-risk" for academic problems. When I asked Hakeem what were some things his teacher does that he does not like he answered, "she thinks you always got to be the bad one in the class that's always guilty. Anything bad happens, your name the first one that come out her mouth." After being asked why he said some of his teachers are not good teachers, Hakeem explained:

> They always be…blaming me for something I didn't do talking
>
> bout they know I did it. I asked her [Mrs. Bean] if I can go to the
>
> bathroom and she talking bout no cuz I'm probably one of the ones
>
> that being drawing graffiti on the stalls. She always blaming stuff
>
> on me and don't have no proof. I cant stand her. [Mrs. Bean] say
>
> she know I will do something wrong. . .last year I punched the wall
>
> in the class for always getting blamed for stuff.

Quincy shared his experience with a school administrator after getting sent to the office for being accused of bullying a student on the bus. He explained a White boy on the

71

bus called him a nigger and he, "punched him in the face." Quincy said, "I got called to the office and they suspended me." I asked him did the student get in trouble for calling him that word and Quincy said, "No. They didn't even ask." We can see from the discipline referral Quincy never was asked why he punched the student; he was simply reprimanded and sent away for recess detention. Later on, Quincy said he feels he gets blamed for a lot of things that happen in the classroom because he did some of those things in his previous grades before the 5th grade.

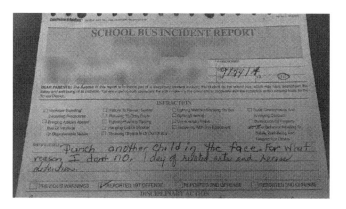

Figure 7.4. Quincy's school bus incident report.

David also believes he is often blamed for bad things that happens in class. David expressed:

> Mrs. Hearn and Mrs. Denver always blame stuff on. . .me and
> Randy. . .we the only two Black boys in class. . .she don't ever say
> nothing to Jake & Toby and they bad White boys that be doing
> stuff too. And. . .we don't ever get called on to be a helper or line
> leaders.

When I asked Trevon to describe his homeroom teacher for me he said:

I don't really like her. She [Mrs. Peeler] always be saying I be

doing something. . .she don't like me or ever call on me or let me be

her student helper cuz she say I'm too bad. Like I don't be doing

nothing and she'll be like go to the ISS room. I don't even care

man.

Trevon also shared with me:

I got in trouble today cuz Kehslie gon say somebody stole her

watch and Mrs. Peeler talking bout she know it was probably me.

She had made me mad cuz I aint take that girl watch. So she gon

send me up to the office till I tell the truth about where I hid it. .

.[also there was this one time] when Jarvis [a White student] trip

me out in the hall and she turn around and write me up for playing

around and I'm the one that got tripped up. And Jarvis didn't even

get written up for what he did.

After I asked him what things makes him angry in his classroom, Samuel

expressed to me, " I. . .don't like getting blamed for stuff I didn't do and teachers that got bad

attitudes." Samuel explained that:

Ooooo like the teacher will hear some noise in the class and won't

see it now, but will turn around so quick and say it was me. And I

tell her it wasn't me and she call me a liar and send me out in the

hallway.

When I asked Samuel if he felt like he often gets blamed for things he doesn't do

he answered:

Oh yea! Like especially cuz I hang with the bad group, we always getting blamed for something. So like about a month ago, Tyleesha gon say that somebody touch her butt outside. I swear to God it wasn't me. I don't even know who did it but Mrs. Beavis gon call me, Shondre, [and] them over and ask us who gon fess up. I was like, 'why you gotta always call my name?'

Samuel expressed during the focus group, "Sometimes we make bad decisions and deserve to get punished but your mistakes shouldn't always be counted against you. Like once your reputation is bad here that's it." Hakeem replied to Samuel's comment by saying, "Even when I try to change my ways, teachers don't see nothing good about me. They only see the bad, or they refuse to see it one."

Interpretation

I believe the participants' experiences certainly details an unjust system where students, notably all Black males, are constantly being questioned, reprimanded, and told they are guilty of various actions because of either their past transgressions, their "at-risk" school label, or unfounded assumptions by school faculty. Even when the participant is involved in a accusation that involves more than one person, as in the story told by Hakeem, it appears the participants are seen automatically as being guilty, being and unworthy of having their side of the story heard. This treatment is perhaps true for Black students, especially males more than any other student demographic at Carolina Elementary. As Ferguson (2001) argued:

> Historically, the existence of African American children has been constituted differently through economic practices, the law, social policy, and visual imagery. This difference has been projected in

an ensemble of images of black youth as not childlike. In the early

decades of this century, representation of black children as

pickaninnies depicted them as verminlike, voracious, dirty,

grinning, animal-like savages. . .Today's representations of black

children still bear traces of these earlier depictions (pgs. 81-82).

Major & Billson (1993) posits, "Being male and black has meant being psychologically castrated—rendered impotent in the economic, political, and social arenas that whites have historically dominated" (p. 1). Isom (2007) noted that Black males must negotiate being African American and male simultaneously creating a combustible combination of intersectionality, especially when African American males internalize the racist and sexist identity assigned to them. This concept of intersectionality may be particular true given that at Carolina Elementary, 204 of the school's 237 suspensions in the 2012-13 school year were males with the remaining 33 suspensions involving females. Within that same data, 144 Blacks, 37 Latinos, and 56 Caucasians were suspended. Thus Black males are disproportionately suspended more than any other school demographic.

Ferguson (2001) argued that expectations, transgressions, and postulations for Black boys mirror expectations for adult males within schools. Ferguson noted that most people identified that children were essentially different from adults, males from females, Blacks from Whites. At the intersection of this complex scope is that African American males are doubly displaced: as Black children, that are not seen as childlike but adultified: and as Black males, that are denied the masculine dispensation constituting White males as being "naturally naughty" and thus are discerned as "willfully bad," manipulative, powerful and cunning (p.80-81).

One particular example of Black males being viewed within this double displacement is when Trevon was sent to the office by his teacher to force a confession from him about stealing another student's watch. The teacher saw Trevon as manipulative, devious, and guilty though she did not articulate any supporting evidence to substantiate her claim other than a postulation. Below is a memo placed in Trevon's file regarding the incident. Unfortunately, this appears to be an reoccurring interaction between Black males and their teachers at Carolina Elementary.

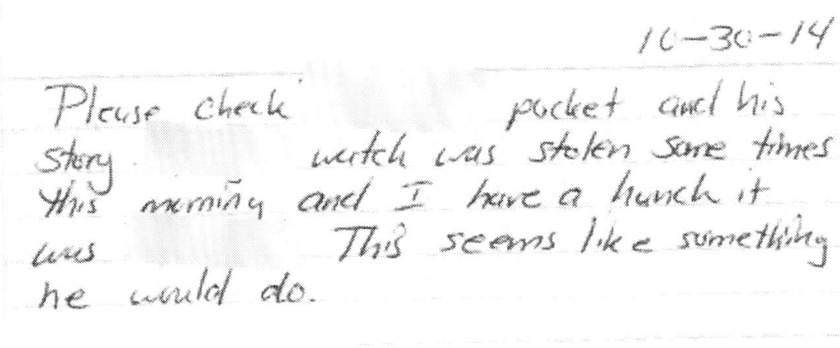

Figure 7.5. *Teacher's note to administrator regarding Trevon's incident.*

Fixing Broken Rules

The rule I broke was

She thinks I stole her watch but I didnt

I broke the rule because

I really didnt break a rule

What should happen because I broke the rule?

She need to find proof that I took it but She cant cuz
I didnt do it

From now on I

_will ___ ask before sue be of me_

Here's my apology

I apologmze for coming to School minding my business and getting
_Bad no body ___ you thinking __ if something goes missing I._

Figure 5.6. *A Fixing Broken Rules worksheet Trevon was asked to write regarding being accused of stealing another student's watch.*

Targeted Exclusion. One pattern that emerged from all the participant interviews was that each participant shared their teacher's routine practice of separating them from the rest of their peers during the school day. The participants explained their teachers usually did this by either positioning their desks away from the other students- usually right by the teacher's desk or by sending them to do work in the hallway or the In-School Suspension room. When I asked Quincy what is the worst part about school he replied, "having to sit by the teacher." Quincy feels this way because, "nobody else has to do it. . .she [Quincy's teacher] said I don't know how to work with others." Hakeem shared a similar story after I asked him why he did not like his teacher Mrs. Bean. Hakeem shared:

>I can't stand her. She be making me line up last in line or making me do group work by myself talking bout, 'I'm the bad influence in the class'. . . I have to sit in a desk right by her desk in class. And I always have to either stand by her in the hallway or be the last one cuz she said she don't want me to influence others, or she will know I will do something wrong. . . [Mrs. Bean will] send you out and you don't even know what you did wrong.

David shared with me he felt as though his teacher was mean and unfair. He said, "sometimes you have to do your work in the hallway or can't be with the rest of the class….like you have to sit by yourself at lunch or work at a workstation by yourself." When I asked David about some "not so good things" his teachers would probably say about him and he said, "I can be a bad influence on others." David explained, "That's the reason why I have to be separated from the class, cuz I like to be a class clown and talk a lot to others and get them in trouble. Mrs. Hearn sends me to [Mrs. Denver] class whenever I be bad."

Teacher Comments:

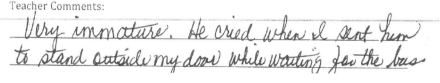

Very immature. He cried when I sent him to stand outside my door while waiting for the bus

Figure **7.7.** *A participant's behavior chart.*

When I asked Samuel what school rules bothers him the most he answered, "having to sit or work by yourself. . .the bad students in our class have to sit in the corner by themselves, and can't participate in group activities, or they will get sent to go sit in the hallway." I asked Samuel if he was included with the group that gets sent out frequently and he replied, "Well kind of. . .I get sent out of class for not doing my work and stuff so she put my desk by her desk cuz she say I be day dreaming or talking too much. I don't like it though." Samuel noted, "you cant see the board from all the places Mrs. Peeler be moving the desk."

Trevon's experience with targeted classroom exclusion actually had an unintended outcome than anticipated. Trevon's social studies teacher shared with me:

> I'm done with Trevon for the year. Some days I can look at him in
> the hallway before he walks in and I can see he is about to be off
> the chain in my classroom. I don't even deal with anymore. I just
> send him to ISS with some work to do to keep my sanity.

Ironically when I asked Trevon what was good about school he mentioned, "going to the ISS room because it gets you outta class and your friends sometimes be in there. I go to sleep when I go there." Thus, what Trevon's teacher believes to be a consequence for him actually was an incentive Trevon began to enjoy.

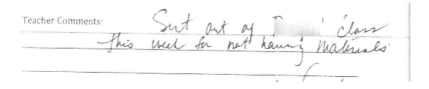

Figure 7.8. *Teacher's note home to Trevon's mother.*

Interpretation

A big, bright blue poster with the words, "All students can learn," is posted outside one of the participant's classroom, yet ironically, I found Hakeem sitting outside his classroom door lying of the floor drawing as his teacher teaches a lesson inside her classroom. Sadly, this appears to be the case for many students who have gained a reputation within this school for being troublemakers. As I walked thru the hallways before and after my interviews I observed many students sitting on the floor outside their classrooms or in the very back of the classrooms while the teacher taught a lesson. Almost all of these students were Black males.

I believe once a student gained the reputation for being a troublemaker within Carolina Elementary teachers began to view these students as unsalvageable. These students are then closely watched, singled out, and excluded from the other students. Furthermore, these "unsalvageable students" are treated as though they are unable to be educated; thus, the energy to correct their behavior or get these students back on task is deemed pointless. Even on occasions when the participants had not broken any rules they were still excluded from participating in group activities or not allowed to engage with their friends as the other students had the privilege of doing. The teachers frequently used targeted exclusion as a form of punishment and preventative management for the participants.

I believe this targeted exclusion served three purposes for the participants' teachers. First, this exclusion provides an opportunity to relieve the teacher of the responsibility of teaching the student. Secondly, targeted exclusion serves as act of humiliation and social marking to the students' peers of being different and finally, this exclusion serves as an act of sanitation from other students so the participant's "badness" cannot rub off on the other students.

The participants readily recognized when they were being isolated from the rest of their classmates and often mentioned this exclusion was one of the practices within school that often made them feel angry or rejected. In fact, all of the teachers that practiced targeted exclusion as a frequent disciplinary routine were listed as the participants' least favorite teacher. This type of isolation resembles a prison system that can afflict deep emotional wounds to students and cause them to feel as though they are prisoners inside their own classroom.

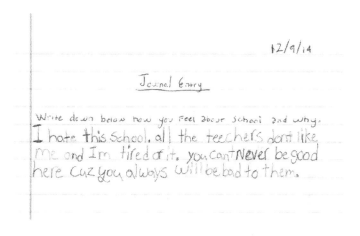

Figure 7.9 *Participant's journal entry regarding his feelings about his teachers.*

Excessive punishment for petty offenses. The final school practice in which the participants experienced marginalization was disproportionate punishment from their teachers. All the participants shared their experiences and agitation in dealing with teachers they felt punished them disproportionately for their offenses. When I asked Hakeem what were the worst parts about school he shared, "Like if you get in trouble…[the teachers] will sit and make it bigger than what it is…that be pissing me off." Hakeem explained:

Say you were talking. They will write you up and say you are disrespectful or refusing to follow their rules, and try to get you suspended. And all you was trying to do was ask somebody what page we were on or something.

Hakeem even shared he receives extra homework from his teachers when he gets in trouble for doing his homework in class. When I asked him why he chooses to do homework in class he responded:

> Like most people do they homework when we just sitting there and we really ain't doing nothing. But she still want you to wait until you get home to do your work, but like for me I have to babysit when I get home and we don't always have lights on in the house, so I try to do it while I can.

Quincy expressed, "Last week I got sent out for blurting out but I had forgot for real." Quincy feels as though, "a lot of rules…really have no point or make sense but you just got to do em." Quincy explained:

> You cant wear hats, you cant chew gum, you cant move, umm you cant never talk, and you got to stand in the 3rd tile in the hall and you gotta walk with your hands behind your back. Like they have no point. Like it don't bother nothing doing that. That's just stuff for you to do and you don't know why… Like that's why I can't really stand school like that, cuz like you come here and get in trouble for everything and you always getting fussed at. I get so tired of that. Like fussing all the time about everything. Like you get in trouble for talking too loud, moving around too much, like anything.

Quincy noted principals should get rid of "stupid rules"…like you can't eat candy in school so why do the teachers pass it out or sell it for Relay for life and you can't bring toys to school but you can buy them from the bookstore?" David shared he was unfairly punished when he mentioned, "[this] morning I had got sent to the office for not doing my morning writing." When I asked David why he did not complete his work he replied, "Cuż Mrs. Hearn have the lights off in the classroom in the morning and I can't see the words on the paper." David also shared last month he received a guidance referral from Mrs. Hearn for having a bad attitude.

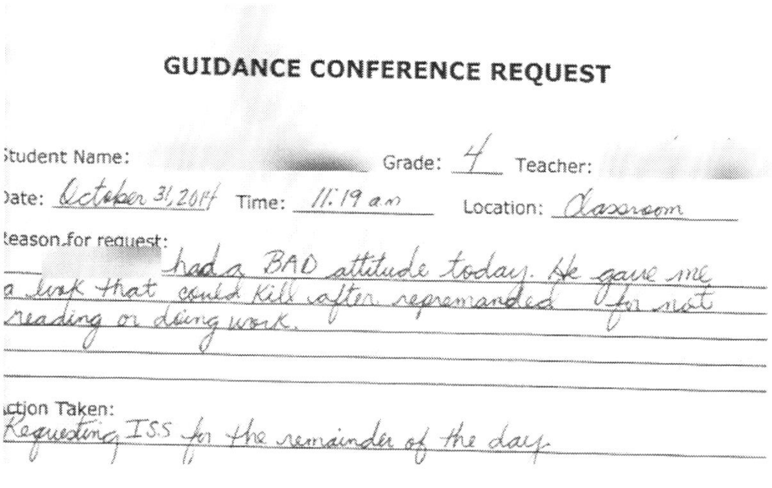

GUIDANCE CONFERENCE REQUEST

Student Name: _____ Grade: 4 Teacher: _____
Date: October 31, 2014 Time: 11:19 am Location: Classroom
Reason for request: had a BAD attitude today. He gave me
a look that could kill after reprimanded for not
reading or doing work.

Action Taken: Requesting ISS for the remainder of the day

Figure 7.10. *Guidance conference request form regarding David having a bad attitude in class.*

David described, "She said I came to school with a bad attitude, and was rude to her, and looked at her like I wanted to kill her." David later expressed he feels as though some of his teachers are mean and unfair because, "Like if you. . .good all day and you do one thing bad, she will call your parents and put you on punishment for a really long time. .

.nobody in the class get that really but me." According to David, "She [Mrs. Hearn & Ms. Denver] don't ever say nothing to Jake & Toby and they bad White boys that be doing stuff too." David feels him and Randy, the only two Black boys in his class, are treated worse than the White boys in class.

When I asked Trevon to describe how he feels about his teachers, Trevon expressed he feels as though his teachers aggravate him. Trevon explained:

They like mess with you about every little thing you do…

Yesterday when Mrs. Zorn gon yell at me in the hallway for

walking with my arms in my shirt talking bout she not gon tell me

anymore to wear my shirt the right way. Say it's December and I,

'shoulda brought a jacket to school if I'm so cold.'

Samuel believes, "every small thing I do…[Mrs. Forrest] always. . .yelling about something I did wrong."

Interpretation

A very disturbing pattern emerged from my data analysis. Carolina Elementary's faculty and staff suspend and expel Black male students more than any other student demographic within the school. Carolina Elementary has failed to adequately prepare over 95% of their Black male students to meet basic performance standards on the state assessment. Noguera (2008) argued the disproportionate involvement of minority students, especially Black and Latino boys, in school discipline problems, suspensions and expulsions comes about when educators use their conscious or unconscious racist or ethnocentric stereotypical beliefs about minority students to interpret their language and behavior. Gregory & Thompson (2010) even concluded Black male students with a history of disciplinary referrals were even more likely to receive negative perceptions and less deference from teachers. There is often a conflict between behaviors adopted by racially diverse students and their White teachers:

> Quite simply, white middle-class teachers and school authorities often perceive provocative walking styles, "rapping," use of slang, expressive hairstyles, excessive use of jewelry, wearing hats (and wearing hats backwards), wearing the belt unbuckled, untied sneakers, and so on as arrogant, rude, defiant, aggressive, intimidating, threatening, and, in general, behaviors not conducive to learning (Tyler Foster, 1986, para. 4).

This was particularly the case when Trevon noted he got in trouble for walking down the hallway with his arms inside his shirt. Though Trevon did not break any school rule, his teacher still found his behavior unacceptable, perhaps compounded by her unconscious racist perceptions of Black males. Subjective perceptions about student behaviors can also be influenced by unconscious or conscious racist beliefs and perceptions such as giving the teacher "a look that could kill" as in David's case. I believe the disproportionate teacher reactions and disciplinary actions to such petty student behavior disrupts students' education and ultimately adds to the academic disparity rates between Black males and their White peers.

SECTION 3

Chapter Eight:

Other Findings & Thoughts

While I provided a thematic analysis of all data obtained during the study in Section two, I draw upon remaining portions of the data I collected to assist me in bringing everything together to answer other of the study's guiding research questions in Section 3. Those research questions were as follows:

1. How do five, pre-adolescent Black male students in a rural elementary school, who have been identified as "at-risk," articulate both their current and past schooling experiences?

2. What do these students' schooling stories reveal about their interactions and engagements with their teachers?

In responding to the research questions, I paid particular attention to the policies, interactions, practices, and behaviors participants disliked, found boring, or incited a strong emotional response. I attended to these factors as well as additional ways the participants articulated their schooling experiences in order to better understand how school may have influenced these African American boys, labeled as "at-risk," to devalue and/or disengage from school. It is important to note my interpretation of the stories my participants (with the exception of David) shared as Black male students were from their own individual schooling experiences without explicit attention to their Blackness and masculinity. Nonetheless, here I offer an analysis of the participants' schooling experiences situated within the lens of

86

Blackness and masculinity and explore the implications of being a Black male within their school.

Research Question 1: How do five, pre-adolescent Black male students in a rural elementary school, who have been identified as "at-risk," articulate both their current and past schooling experiences?

I value school but I don't like it. The participants generally expressed going to school was valuable and useful for obtaining an education. Though they valued the institution of schooling for the potential education they could receive from attending, they did not like the dynamics of their schooling process. The participants' efforts to do well in school was not their assimilation and acceptance of the schooling process, but rather their means to reap the societal benefits associated with becoming a high school graduate. Participants such as Trevon expressed, "I really don't like coming to school but I do cuz momma say you can't do anything in life without an education. I guess that's why I try to keep coming so I can go to college and take care of my family one day." Trevon explained, "school is boring. You sit all day and do packets and projects all day." He further noted he does not get a lot of respect in school because, "people think I'm bad and that I'm dumb." When I asked Hakeem if he would stop attending school if he could he responded, "Yea cuz I don't feel like waking up at 6 o' clock in the morning plus school suck." Hakeem explained, "I mean it don't all the way suck. Like I like to learn and be with my friends. It's just when somebody be messing with me that I don't like it or it be boring."

Quincy had similar sentiments regarding school. He said:

"I don't really like school but I don't wanna stay at home all day

either. You need to go to school so you can go to college. . .Like

some days at school be fun when you have assemblies and you

learn things or be with your friends but some days its aggravating."

Quincy feels as though school is aggravating because he does not learn things at school every day, but rather does busywork like reading or filling out worksheets. When I asked Samuel if he would stop attending school if he could he said:

"No cuz I want to graduate from high school and go to college and

do music for my career. If I didn't have to finish school and could

start my music career right away I probably wouldn't come though.

My grandma says doing good in school will eventually pay off so I

guess that's one of the reasons why I try to do good."

When I asked David if he would stop attending school if could he said, "No because I want to learn and go to college." David explains, however, school is, "really hard and you will fail your classes or get in trouble easily."

These participants' stories illustrate an antithesis to educational research that posits African American youth do not place a high value on education and oppose structures and systems of education (Benson, 2000; Fordham & Ogbu, 1986; Harper, 2009b; Shakespeare, 2012). The participants in this study did value education and the societal privileges associated with getting a "good education." They saw school as the means to obtaining a "good education," thus, enabling themselves with the possibility of attending college, getting a good job, or being able to take of their families in the future. The participants did not however, place value on the process of schooling.

By schooling I refer to Shujaa's (1994) definition of schooling as a "process intended to perpetuate and maintain society's existing power relations and the institutional structures that support those arrangements" (p. 15). This of course is not interchangeable with the term education, which in contrast to the term schooling, is "the process of transmitting from one generation to the next knowledge of values, aesthetics, spiritual beliefs, and all things that give a particular cultural orientation its uniqueness" (p.15). The participants' feelings regarding their schooling experiences are more aligned to educational research such as Harris (2006), who argued not only is oppositional culture to education not true for all Black male students but their beliefs regarding social equity via education is actually high . In fact, participants in his longitudinal study actually believed one could transcend poverty and social disadvantage through high rates of educational attainment.

School is monotonous, uninteresting, and dull. Throughout my data collection, the participants frequently expressed school is boring, monotonous, restrictive, and full of busy work. When I asked Hakeem to express the reasons he believes students either dislikes school or wish they did not have to attend school he explained:

> Peep this, like school real boring to them. Like nothing really
> interest them at school and they feel like school is a bunch of busy
> work and they don't do good at sitting and working by themselves
> in the quiet all day. Some people do better at like the alternative
> school. Quaz [and] them got sent there from the middle school and
> they like it better cuz they don't do things like a regular school.
> Some boys be trying to get enough write-ups so they can get sent
> there too.

David mentioned he normally does worksheet packets in his classroom after every lesson. David said, "It be a lot of them and it be stuff on them that you never been taught before how to do. They be real boring." When I asked Quincy if he learns things at school everyday he responded "no." Quincy stated the days at school when he is not learning he is, "reading, doing work, . . . like them packets," work he feels is, "stuff to keep you quiet and busy." When I asked Hakeem what made school boring to him he said "having to sit all day in the cold and. . .having to do a bunch of worksheets and reading." In fact, Hakeem's describes one of his four major classes as fun because, "we don't have to do a bunch of worksheets in there." Hakeem says "not having to do worksheets" is what makes him happy in his classroom.

Some of the participants also mentioned their discontent with teachers who predominantly used visual and auditory modalities and catered to the verbal and linguistic intelligences throughout their classroom activities and assessment. Samuel shared with me he believed some students begin to dislike school because:

> You can't really do the stuff you really like doing or that you're
> really good at very often. Like for me I like music and I'm good at
> it, but I only come to music once a week. See. . .I use music all the
> time, cuz sometimes I be thinking about the music notes in math to
> help me figure out them fractions and stuff. That help me stay
> focused and like math. But say like somebody that really like cars
> but they don't ever really learn much about how cars are built in
> science or something. That person not really gonna want to do the
> work or focus on it cuz it's never fun to them.

Samuel, now in the fifth grade, also shared how much he enjoyed Mr. Simuel's class in the fourth grade. Mr. Simuel was Samuel's first male teacher. Samuel exclaimed:

> He was great! I learned a lot in his class. His class was real fun;
> we would make stuff, go on field trips, some of his Frat brothers
> would come to the school and show us steps. . . he was Black too. .
> .he would rap for us and talk about rappers and things we liked.
> That was the best teacher of my life. I was smart in his class.

When I asked Samuel why he felt smart in Mr. Simuel's class he said, "Cuz that was the only year I almost made A/B honor roll. Like for our science project he let me sing a song about the different cloud types instead of doing a test." Hakeem also shared his desire of being allowed to use his interests and other ways of learning in the classroom more often too. Hakeem said he would like to "have all the Brothers' Keepers[1] in the same class" because they were all "Black and boys," something that made him more comfortable. Hakeem said he preferred this type of class arrangement because:

> We all like the same type of music and sports and stuff and we do
> those things in. . .our work. Like. . .we wrote about what would we
> do if we could be the host of 106th and Park last week during our
> journal time, or we could do jumping jacks during multiplication
> tournament. Oh, and we can make a rap song as a project for the
> Reconstruction era we learned about.

---

[1] Brothers' Keepers is a mentoring program at Carolina Elementary for African American male students. Students in the program meet everyday with the program director and volunteer Black males from the community. Three of the participants from the study are members of the Brothers' Keepers program.

The participants also echoed their disdain for the school-wide practice of having to be silent for most of the day. David shared, "we normally have to be silent all day." When I asked him does he ever have time to talk during the day he said:

"Yea at recess but I don't have them a lot. I normally have structured recess. . .[because] I probably start saying something to somebody at my table. Like we sit at tables of six so it's kind of hard to sit there the whole time and not say anything to anyone."

Quincy shared having to go to Ms. Colleton class is one of the worst parts about school because he feels, "She [is] aggravating. She always telling you what to do. . .You can't never talk in her class or move." In contrast, Quincy stated Mr. Reeve's class was one of the best parts of school because, "you can work in groups and work on the floor and talk."

Trevon expressed his opinion on the school's silence rule by stating, "Its not about like just talking, like free time talking, but sometimes if you talk with a partner they can help you understand it. . .Like when I. . .worked with Jasmine I. . .understood it better." The participants also articulated in their own ways they feel as though their body movement is closely monitored and controlled throughout the school day. Samuel says himself, and other boys in his class, normally gets in trouble for "being up out of [their] seat" because "we at the pencil sharpener too long or just walking around for no reason." Samuel further explained that he gets bored in class when "[we] have to sit in our desk for the whole time" and believes the ability to move about in the classroom is something that could help him stay awake. Samuel expressed his value of moving by stating:

Recess be the time that I get to stretch my bones cuz when we get in the classroom we can't move and the teachers act like they want you to be a robot and don't ever move. And then the teachers be asking you why you stretching and I be saying, cuz my bones hurt

so much from sitting that long.

Quincy even feels as though teachers' expectations for body movement are "rules that don't really have a point." Quincy said, "you cant move, . . .and you got to stand in the third tile in the hall and you gotta walk with your hands behind your back." During the focus group, Quincy reiterated his disdain by saying:

I don't like them rules that tell you, you got to walk a certain way,

or sit a certain way in the desk. Like they try to tell you everything

now. . .like they gon tell you how to sneeze soon.

When I asked him what he does when he sits for a long period of time he said, "I get bored and start to do stuff like draw or sleep." Quincy further exclaimed:

That's why I can't really stand school. . .cuz like you come here

and get in trouble for everything and you always getting fussed at.

I get so tired of that. Like fussing all the time about everything.

Like you get in trouble for. . .moving around too much, like

anything.

Analysis

I believe the participants' intersectional identities as Black males impacts their feelings and perspectives regarding school. As noted before in the previous chapter, homeroom[2] classrooms with the highest population of African American and male students

---

[2] Carolina Elementary students are all grouped and assigned to a teacher's homeroom class. This grouping remains fixed throughout the school day and moves between classroom teachers and functions (lunch, recess, math, social-studies,

are usually remedial classes taught by teachers within Carolina Elementary with a reputation for being strict disciplinarians. On the contrary, homeroom classes that offer more rigorous curricula are populated by mostly White female students and taught by teachers who serve as grade level chairpersons with reputations for having high-test scores. Though there is no official policy on what types of students teachers will mostly receive in their homerooms, there is a long running saying amongst the faculty at Carolina Elementary to "get high test scores or become the grade level chair so you can teach the gifted class." Indeed, a fifth grade teacher who is a self-proclaimed strict disciplinarian stated to me:

> I've been here 16 years and all of my classes are the Black kids that's either bad as hell or they not on grade level. I know they do it cuz some of the other teachers can't handle em like me, cuz you can hear a rat piss on cotton in my class! But I'm like damn, if you keep giving me the remedial kids of course I'm never going to get the high test scores!

Thus, the participants' feelings that school is monotonous, restrictive, and uninteresting can be linked to their placement in a remedial homeroom class that are mostly taught by teachers who employ strict disciplinary measures. Kozol (2005) asserts a trend in schools that serve poor communities is the use of Skinnerian Curriculum. The Skinnerian Curriculum, as it is colloquially referred to, takes its inspiration from the ideas of B. F. Skinner who promotes proponents of scripted rote-and-drill curricula where the aim is

---

music, etc.) at the same time. Students rotate between five teachers each school day to receive instruction. Whatever subject student's homeroom teacher is assigned (ELA, social studies, math, or science) also serves as the student's first class of the day.

"faultless communication" between "the teacher, who is the stimulus," and "the students, who respond." Kozol (2005) noted:

> The introduction of Skinnerian approaches, which are commonly employed in penal institutions and drug-rehabilitation programs, as a way of altering the attitudes and learning styles of Black and Hispanic children is provocative. . . Although generically described as school reform, most of these practices and policies are targeted primarily at poor children of color; and although most educators speak of these agendas in broad language that sounds applicable to all, it is understood that they are valued chiefly as responses to perceived catastrophe in deeply segregated and unequal schools. . .The intense theatricality of the educators while teaching scripted lessons, with no creativity and rampant reiteration, stifles dynamic and responsive teaching. Simply put, a child's silence and ability to sit still does not mean that the child is learning (p. 64-66).

Furthermore, excessive reliance on worksheets as a teaching mechanism can be a component of culturally unresponsive pedagogy. Hurley (2010) asserts teaching from a worksheet alone or developing teaching mechanisms garners little interaction between teachers and their students, causing a poor affects on cultural diverse students. For example, those who tend to work in a more collectivist, relationship driven nature may have difficulty learning from worksheets where the focus is to learn alone.

Morgan (2007) also concluded there are shifts in the way teachers instruct students by the fourth grade. Unlike the earlier years where teachers encouraged social interactions in the classrooms, by the fourth grade classrooms become a more static, lecturing environment. This change in teaching approach, from an informal, learning-by-doing style to the more structured, sit-down-and-listen setup, is toughest on male students who tend to be more active than girls in the elementary grades. And for Black boys, a teacher's reactions to these high energy levels may be compounded by racialized assumptions, as noted by Morgan, which usually results in Black boys being recommended for special education (2007).

I believe the intense surveillance of the participants' bodies are also because of other factors such as race and social class. Kaba (2010) asserts the emphasis on the orderly movement of students and their obedience to strict codes of conduct is also important both to schools' operational functioning and to their societal functions. Critical scholars such as Foucault (1977) and Bowles & Gintis (1976) have argued strict disciplinary regimens in working class schools help to promote smooth and voluntary transitions into an industrial workplace that tightly regulates and subordinates laborers.

Recent empirical research by Nance (2013) indicated schools serving higher proportions of minority and low-income students are more likely to implement harsh, intense security conditions than other schools such as heavy restrictions on movement, having law enforcement present on campus, conducting random sweeps for contraband, and installing security cameras. The U.S. Department of Education (2012) even noted schools that rely on intense surveillance methods often have poor school climates that are detrimental to student learning and positive student growth, meaning poor students and students of color often do not enjoy the same educational experiences that other students do. Furthermore, the use of intense surveillance methods is a component of a larger, more complex problem called the school-to-prison pipeline that disproportionately affects Black males than any other student demographic in our nation (Nance, 2013).

For some of the participants like Samuel and Hakeem, the presence of a Black male teacher in their life was very salient to them. Monroe & Obidah (2004) argued the probability of racial and cultural relevancy and teacher-student cultural synchronization becomes greatly increased when Black male students have Black male teachers. Milner further asserts Black male teachers can enrich the lives of many diverse students because they possess colorful stories of history filled with lessons on strength, oppression, success, and life experiences. Educational researchers Thomas-El (2006), Simmons (2011), & Bridges (2011) even noted many African American male teachers not only see themselves in their students, but are also invested in the profession to help assist African American male students understand and navigate a racist society. As such, I believe the implications of having a Black male teacher in the lives of Black male students can be an empowering, positive experience for students.

Research Question 1 Response Summary

The two salient ways the five participants articulated both their current and past schooling experience is that: a) they value education but not school and b) school is monotonous, dull and restrictive. The participants in large, believes that getting a "good education" is important and necessary to be able to go to college and obtain a "good job," however, they do not like school. To them, school is monotonous, dull, and restrictive. The participants articulated much of their school time is spent completing packets of worksheets with little guidance from their teachers. School wide expectations for students to remain silent and still throughout most of the school day also contributes to their dislike for the schooling process. The participants generally expressed their desire for their teachers to include diverse ways of assessing and teaching students such letting students respond with jumping jacks during multiplication questions or being allowed to write a song about a topic instead of taking a paper-based assessment.

Research Question 2: What do these students' schooling stories reveal about their interactions and engagements with their teachers?

For the participants, school is a warzone between them and most of the teachers who instruct them. Many of the participants revealed to me they were extremely bothered whenever a teacher interacted with them aggressively through physical or verbal contact. I asked Quincy what he thought would be some reasons why some students either disliked school or wished they did not have to come back anymore. Quincy responded by saying "Like the teachers will point they finger in your face and walk up on you like they about to whip you or something." Quincy further suggested, "Don't treat students bad. . .don't be pulling on them to get in line or getting in they face yelling. They [teachers] wouldn't want it done to them. Let one of us do it to them. They would kick us out so fast."

Samuel, now in the fifth grade, believed his second-grade teacher did not like him because:

"Ms. Kennedy would say I don't study or that I was being lazy. . . and shout in my face. . .I would get mad and shout at her and say I do work. . . and she would send me out."

Samuel also listed "when teachers get in your face and be pointing and screaming at you," as one of the things that makes him angry at school. According to Samuel:

They [teachers] come to the school with a bad attitude and want to talk to us any kind of way and expect for us to just sit and take it. Like if we get an attitude we get sent out but if they do when we asking a simple question than it's ok. Sometimes I just don't even say nothing in class cuz I don't feel like dealing with em.

The participants' stories also revealed they felt as though they were unprepared to be academically successful in their classrooms. When I asked Samuel which classes is he most bored in, he answered, "Probably science and math cuz . . .it ain't never really taught how to do it in a way you can understand. You just do work and get a bunch of grades but you don't know what you're doing." When I asked Samuel why he does not ask for help he responded, "if I don't understand something. . .I sit there and try to figure it out but by then I normally get bored and start doing something else." He explained, "sometimes in Mrs. Forrest class I don't ask her nothing cuz I don't too much like her. . .[because] you just don't feel like getting told you should have been paying attention before they help you." When I asked Trevon what his most boring classes are he said:

> Science and social studies cuz all they do is talk and pass out work.
> They don't really even explain how to do it really. They just be
> reading out the book. Especially Ms. Buyer. She always reading
> stuff out the book.

I later asked Quincy to describe his experiences from on his previous school he attended. Quincy described the school as "aggravating" because:

> She [his math teacher] didn't even teach you cuz like the teachers
> there don't really help you. She like, would give you a worksheet
> and don't tell you how to do it. And then she'll like, call my name
> cuz I used to sit there and draw on the desk or something cuz I
> didn't know how to do it.

It is important to note there were some instances from the participants' stories that revealed the participants did have positive relationships and interactions with some of their teachers, notably, their White teachers. When I asked Hakeem to tell me the best parts about school he replied, "They got some great teachers that will look out for you and give you second chances. . .Like you, Mrs. Cayers [White female teacher], and Coach [White male teacher]." Hakeem says these three teachers are good to him because, "they care about me. . .yall (myself included) give me second chances and yall help me out and nice to me. Like yall say I'm smart or I'm a leader." Hakeem later explained Mrs. Cayers is real nice to him because:

> She helps me when I don't understand something. She tell me good things about me. She gives me second chances if I mess up and let me be her helper. Like if I lose a paper she will give me another paper without a big problem and still give me a chance to get a 100. Her class fun. We can move around and talk in there and we don't do a bunch of worksheets in there. We still got a lot of reading though.

Samuel says the best part about school to him is there are some teachers who look out for him and makes sure he staying on the right track. He explained:

> Well yall ask me how I'm doing, remind me about assignments, and give me second chances to make up my work, or to take something over. Not all my teachers do that, but like you and Mrs. Forrest [Black female teacher] does that.

When I asked Samuel to describe his current favorite teacher he said, "She's loving and caring and she likes to tells stories about her past. She's a big White lady with short blond hair. . .umm she loves to talk a lot." When I asked Quincy what were some of the best parts about his school he replied:

"Mr. Reeves' [White male] math class. . .he's funny, and he gives

you second chances if you mess up and he talk to you and tell you

why you in trouble. In his class you get to toss football with him."

David shared with me his favorite teacher is Ms. Willette (Black female teacher) because, "she takes her time and explains things to me. She tells me I'm smart and give me gifts when I do good."

<u>Analysis</u>

Students' sense of their teacher-student relationship at school is a key component in contemporary educational theories of academic motivation and engagement (Coleman, 2007; Collier, 2002; Kafele, 2009; Stipek, 2002). When students experience a sense of belonging at school and feel as though they have supportive relationships with teachers and classmates, they are more likely to be motivated to participate actively and appropriately in the life of the classroom (Anderman & Anderman, 1999; Gay, 2000; Howard, 2008). Students' sense of belonging at school has also been linked both to their engagement and academic success (Skinner, Zimmer-Gembeck, & Connell, 1998). This literature corroborates with participants' experiences of feeling disconnected from most of their teachers as an influence to their disengagement and/or devaluing of school.

According to Hill (2004), positive relations with teachers in the classroom and between home and school appear to be less common for low-income and racial minority children than for higher income, White students. Research executed around the relationships between White teachers and Black students most often are associated with White teachers having deficit assumptions or turbulent experiences with Black students (King, 1994; Lewis, Hancock, James, & Larke, (2006); Mitchell, 1998; Quiocho & Rios, 2000). However, there are also several research studies that present successful examples of White teachers educating

Black students (Boucher, 2013, Coleman, 2007, Ladson-Billings, 1994, Sleeter & Soriano, 2012).

Much of the research that posit some White teachers' view Black students from a deficit perspective is compounded with additional research that suggested the gap between White teachers and Black students is exacerbated by powerful social conditioning that cultivates actual negative perceptions about Black students (Douglas, Lewis, Scott & Garrison-Wade, 2008). Boykin (1992) and Scheurich (1993) noted some White teachers work from within a hegemonic, Western, epistemological framework, which often predisposes them to have lower expectations of Black students and a lack of respect for the students' families and primary culture. Therefore, the possibility of effective teaching Black students by these types of teachers is greatly reduced.

Multiple factors can often contribute to the quality of student–teacher relationships. In an investigation of male students relationships with their teachers compared to their female counterparts, Saft & Pianta, (2001) concluded boys' relationships with teachers are characterized by less closeness and more conflict as teachers found boys to be less conforming and self-regulated than girls. Ferguson's (2001) even argued expectations, transgressions, and postulations for Black boys mirror expectations for adult males within schools. Ferguson noted most people identified that children were essentially different from adults, males from females, Blacks from Whites. At the intersection of this complex scope is that African American males are doubly displaced: as Black children, that are not seen as childlike but adultified: and as Black males, who are denied the masculine dispensation constituting White males as being "naturally naughty"-thus Black males are discerned as "willfully bad," manipulative, powerful, and cunning (p.80-81).

Research Question 2 Response Summary

The participants' stories reveal their relationships and interactions with many of their teachers are often turbulent and negative. The participants shared their teachers routinely interacted with them aggressively thru physical and verbal acts such as teachers putting their finger in students' faces and yelling, snatching items from students, grabbing forcefully on students, or screaming at students. The participants also shared they felt as though their negative relationships with some of their teachers impacted their ability to be academically successful in the classroom. Despite these dominant, negative themes regarding participants and their teachers, their stories did detail some of the participants had positive relationships and interactions with teachers that they deeply valued. Notably, some of these positive teacher-student relationships were with White female teachers.

The primary purpose of this study was to illuminate, and subsequently gain a deeper understanding of the past and current schooling experiences of five pre-adolescent African American males, labeled as "at-risk." Further, throughout this study, I sought to understand the specific teacher interactions and school policies that influence these five participants to disengage and/or devalue school. It is clear the negative dynamics with the participants' teachers and school plays a pivotal role in shaping their beliefs and feelings towards school.

In summarizing, the boys' social class, gender, and race, amongst other factors, impacts how school practices are shaped and how educators interact with students. The majoritarian story from this study is participants' relationships and interactions with many of their teachers are often turbulent and negative. The participants shared their teachers routinely interacted with them aggressively thru physical and verbal acts such as teachers putting their finger in students' faces and yelling, snatching items from students, grabbing forcefully on students, or screaming at students. The participants even expressed many of the adults with the school building often assumed they were guilty or devious whenever a student violation occurred, sometimes even without evidence. The participants also shared they felt as though their negative relationships with some of their teachers impacted their ability to be academically successful in the classroom.

Unconscious and conscious racialized school practices by teachers particularly marginalized African American males as well. The participants shared their frustration with teachers' over-policing and hypercriminalization of the unofficial school policy of sagging pants. The participants in the fifth grade also expressed their English teachers prohibited students' use of Black English or Ebonics in the classroom. Students that use Black English are subjected to disciplinary sanctions such as loss of student recess time, point reductions in class grades, or even detention. Teachers' perception of the participant and the participant's school reputation also played a major role that resulted in the participants' excessive punishment for petty offenses and the act of routine separation of participants during the school day from their peers.

Larger institutional practices that impact marginalized groups across the U.S. are also revealed in the participants' stories. School expectations for students to be silent and still for much of the school day are what Critical scholars such as Foucault (1977) and Bowles & Gintis (1976) argue, is in place so working class schools can help promote smooth and voluntary transitions into an industrial workplaces that tightly regulates and subordinates laborers. Other monotonous "drill kill curricula" the participants often orate about are characteristic of a systemic institutional practice that Kozol (2006) asserts is often in place in poor school districts of marginalized groups. The participants' stories demonstrate a powerful, yet disconcerting illustration of how educational institutions continue to reproduce

societal inequities and racism behind the facade of equal treatment and opportunity.

Chapter Nine:

Recommendations for Future Reforms

To the real question, "How does it feel to be a problem?" I answer seldom a word. And yet, being a problem is a strange experience. –**W.E.B. DU Bois,** *Souls of Black Folk*

The five participants, all with diverse personalities and perspectives, shared their poignant, first-hand experiences as young Black boys at Carolina Elementary School. Their sagacious stories of their schooling journey, filled with turmoil, isolation, anger, and frustration with being misunderstood, helped me to see their resilience and hope for better times. Their experiences, while certainly not monolithic in nature, became a nuanced story that illuminated explicit teaching interactions and school practices that marginalized Black boys labeled as "at-risk" at Carolina Elementary. Their collective narrative reminds us that factors such as the color of your skin, the way you dress, the way you speak, your gender, and the neighborhood where you live, among others, are still salient reasons for being discriminated against, excluded, and marginalized within our nation's schools. These factors, combined with teachers' conscious and unconscious biases and assumptions, school labels of students, and the ever-driving need to improve test scores, creates a combustible fate for the most vulnerable, the student. In this chapter, I offer my brief recommendations for school reform:

Recommendations When Attempting to Curb Discipline Problems

Not Effective

- Be Punitive
- Focus on all the negatives on the students
- Increase focus on punishments
- Punish their parents
- Get stricter, doing more of what doesn't work
- Consult with no one
- Retreat to one's authority and power

Most effective

- Celebrate successes and small gains
- See the good of the student
- Manage your own reaction
- Gather info about the environment & disposition (what they brought to school)
- Consider more than 2 ways to look at what happened to be accurate & nonbiased
- Get the facts/ask questions/**listen, listen, listen**
- Work in partnership
- Seek cultural consultation
- See misbehavior as a opportunity to teach/model the correct behavior
- Understand that these students are not helpless

Be Color Bold in you Reflective Questions?

- What do we know is currently being done about this?
- What can I do to work towards reversing the statistical trends of Black males at our school?
- What can we do as a school to reverse the statistical trends of Black males at our school?
- How would I describe the boys that I teach?
- How would I describe the African American boys that I teach?
- In what areas do I struggle with this demographic of students?

My Challenge to Educators Reading this Text:

Think about one African American male in your classroom that has exhibited one or more of these characteristics:

- Low scores on the State Standardized test
- Poor academic performance on classroom-level assessments related to the state's academic standards
- Generally displays a lack of effort or interest in their academic work
- Have a history of discipline problems leading to suspension, expulsion, and/or probation
- Showing or expressing feelings of being disconnected from the school environment

Take on this one student (could be more) and try to build a closer relationship.
1. Identify students for whom you have low expectations or issues with
2. Identify similarities in students
3. Identify differential treatment of that group
4. Treat that group the same as high expectancy students

Implications for Reform in School Practices

I believe the data from this book has implications for reforming several school practices. School officials must first examine their school's data to assess if there is an unequal representation that affects a particular racial, gender, class group or students who reflect a combination of those social indicators. Carolina Elementary, the research site used for this research study, had several unequal representations of students in a variety of areas. For example, Black males represented almost half of Carolina Elementary's special education program while White females populated almost 80% of the school's gifted and talented program. Black students, especially males, also represented nearly 70% of the students who were suspended and were also the only demographic (Black males) the school failed to help meet any of the tested subjects on the State's standardized test. From a litany of national and state data within the past decade, unequal distribution for Black males similar to what has occurred at Carolina Elementary, is being experienced in other schools across the nation.

If we reject notions that assert various races are genetically inferior with low intelligence capacities and high urges of criminality, we, as educators and stakeholders, must examine schooling practices that over or under-represents groups of students in various areas such as gifted and talented placements, student suspension rates, or standardized test rates. Nieto (2009) even contends that deep-seated, often unconscious, prejudices held by teachers, administrators, and policy makers often manifest in the education structures of our schools and the education experiences of our students. She argues that the social ills of racism, sexism, and other types of discrimination are embedded in schools' practice and design as much as they are in society at large. Thus, this discrimination is not only revealed through the actions (often resulting from unconscious prejudices) of teachers, but through student outcomes such as dropout rates, college attendance, and other indicators of educational failure or success.

Drawing on data from this study, I argue that the following school practices unequally impacted and marginalized a specific race, gender, and/or class within Carolina Elementary, particularly young Black male students: a) the intense restriction and monitoring of body movement and talking, b) the policing of sagging pants, c) the prohibition of Ebonics or Black English, d) the lack of incorporation of different learning modalities, and e) the proliferation of office referrals under the monitoring of substitute teacher. Though these practices may be unique to Carolina Elementary, school officials can use data from this study to monitor similar classroom and school rules and practices that may reflect racial, gender, and social class biases within their school.

Implications for Professional Development

The data from this study can certainly be used for professional development for any practicing administrator, teacher, or school. As Howard (2013) noted, the narrative, from multiple sources, paints a disturbing account of the overall manner in which many schools are falling woefully short in meeting the needs of Black males. However, too often the focus is placed on how we can "fix" Black males rather than how we can equip schools and teachers to better meet the educational needs of Black males. Rather than providing education practitioners with broad, ideological approaches for addressing the needs of Black males, this study offers practitioners with valuable information regarding young black males' schooling experiences upon which they can immediately reflect. Further, they can actively choose to monitor, modify, or eliminate detrimental practices, policies, and behaviors within their school cultures that reflect monolithic deficit assumptions about, and biases against, their Black male students.

It is my hopes this book can inspire similar, on-going professional development workshops throughout our nation's schools. It was not my intent to provide a simplistic or prescriptive account of how to best understand and teach Black males. Rather, the intent of this study is to encourage educators to be reflective about their biases, assumptions, and values; and to understand that all students' experiences and voices are important and need to be heard. I believe it is critical to understand that, while educational researchers, teachers, and stakeholders may have invaluable input in helping teachers meet the needs of all students, it is the students themselves who have the most important input. After all, they are the ones living the experience day-to-day!

Concluding Thoughts

It is my hope this book engages educators and other stakeholders in critical dialogue. It is this dialogue that I pray will decrease the number of Black male students sitting in the office or hallway each day and increase the number of Black male students marching in cap and gowns, receiving diplomas and degrees. Though teachers cannot be blamed for the totality of performance gaps for Black children, we do play an important and vital role in our students' school experience. At times, our classroom environments can inspire students to achieve at prodigious rates or discourage students to the point that they may consider dropping out of school or mentally "tapping out."

This research is intended not just for White teachers of Black male students, but Black teachers, Asian teachers, Hispanic teachers, and so forth. This book has even transformed my teaching and I am a Black male who has years of experience with working with young Black youth. The point is, regardless of a teacher's race, we all must continuously understand and check our biases and monitor our behaviors and actions to ensure that we, as teachers, do all we can to be catalysts of success for ALL students. Only then do I believe we can actually hold true to Rita Pierson's words, "Every child deserves a champion – an adult who will never give up on them, who understands the power of connection and insists that they become the best that they can possibly be."

"They see me. Good teachers they don't like look past me but they see me. Its like they see me for me and not what they think I am or what they want me to be."

Above is an example of the possibilities and greatness of "Black boy magic!" I met this young man in the 3rd grade and he became a part of my mentoring program, Brothers' Keeper. In 2018, he graduated Salutatorian of his middle school class! He is destined for success!

References

Ahram, R., Stembridge, A., Fergus, E., & Noguera, P (2011). Framing Urban School Challenges: The Problems to Examine When Implementing Response to Intervention, RTI.

Alvidrez, J., & Weinstein, R. S. (1999). Early teacher interceptions and later student academic achievement. Journal of Educational Psychology, 91(4), 731–746.

Alward, M. (2006). Is Your Child's Teacher a Bully? A Better Child.

America's Cradle to the Prison Pipeline. Children's Defense Fund. Washington, D.C. 2007

Anderson, E. (2008). *Against the wall: Poor, young, Black, and male*. Philadelphia: University of Pennsylvania Press

Anderman, E. M., Maehr, M. L., & Midgley, C. (1999).Declining motivation after the transition to middle school: Schools can make a difference. *Journal of Research and Development in Education, 32*, 131-147.

Anyon, J. (2005). *Radical possibilities: Public policy, urban education, and a new social movement.* New York: Routledge.

Au, K. H., and Mason, J.M. (1981) Social organizational factors in learning to read: The balance of rights hypothesis. *Reading Research Quarterly* 17:115-152.

Au, W. (Ed.). (2009). *Rethinking multicultural education: Teaching for racial and cultural justice*. Milwaukee: Rethinking Schools, Ltd.

Baber, C. (2010). Report: 5 percent of college students are black males. Observer-Dispatch.

Bell D. A. (1992). *Faces at the Bottom of the Well*. New York, NY: Basic Books.

Benson, K. F. (2000). Constructing academic inadequacy: African American athletes' stories of schooling. The Journal of Higher Education, 71(2), 223-246.

Billings, G. (2005). *Beyond the big house: African American educators on teacher education*. New York: Teacher College Press.

Brantlinger, E. (2003). Dividing classes: How the middle class negotiates and rationalizes school. New York, NY: RoutledgeFalmer.

Brown, A. L. (2009). "Brothers gonna work it out": Understanding the pedagogic perfor- mance of African American male teachers working with African American male students.
Urban Review, 41, 416–435.

Building Blocks for Youth, 2004. "Zero Tolerance" Fact Sheet, www.build ingblocksforyouth.org/ issues/zerotolerance/facts.html.

Books, S. (2004). *Poverty and schooling in the U.S.: Contexts and consequences.* Mahway, NJ: Erlbaum.

Boutte, G. S. (2008). Teaching Students Who Speak African American Language. Language, Culture, and Community in Teacher Education. Lawrence Erlbaurn Associates. New York, NY.

Buyse, E., Verschueren, K., Verachtert, P., & Van Damme, J. (2009). Predicting school adjustment in early elementary school: Impact of teacher-child relationship quality and relational classroom climate. *Elementary School Journal, 110*(2), 119-141.

Caton, M. (2012). Black male perspectives on their educational experiences in high school. *Urban Education, 47*(6).

Crenshaw, K. (1989). Demarginalizing the intersection of race and sex. *University Chicago Legal Files*, pp. 139–167.

Cochran-Smith, M. (2004). Knowledge, skills, and experiences for teaching culturally diverse learners: A perspective for practicing teachers. In J. J. Irvine (Ed.), *Criti- cal knowledge for diverse teachers and learners* (pp. 27-87). Washington, DC: American Association of Colleges for

Cobb, D. (2012). Throwing out the culturally unresponsive cookie cutter. Canadian Journal of Action Research. 13 (3) 3-18.

Coleman, B. (2007). Successful white teachers of black students: teaching across racial lines in urban middle school science classrooms. Unpublished doctoral dissertation. Amherst: University of Massachusetts

Collier, M. (2002). Changing the Face of Teaching: Preparing Educators for Diverse Settings. Teacher Education Quarterly. 4(1) 49-56.

Damle, R. (2006). Investigating the Impact of Substitute Teachers on Student Achievement: A Review of Literature. Research Deployment and Accountability.

Darling-Hammond, Linda & Post, Laura (2000). A Notion at Risk: Preserving Public Education as an Engine for Social Mobility, The Century Foundation, 127-167.

Darling-Hammond, L. (2006). The flat earth and education: How America's commitment to equity will determine our future. *Educational Researcher, 36*, 318–334.

Darling-Hammond, L. (2010). *The flat world and education: How America's commitment to equity will determine our future*. New York, NY: Teachers College Press.

Davis, J. (2003). Early schooling and academic achievement of African American males. Urban Education, 38(5), 515–537.

Dee, T. S. (2004). The race connection: Are teachers more effective with students who share their ethnicity? *Education Next*, 2004 (2), 52-59.

Delpit, L. (1998) What should teacher's do? Ebonics and culturally responsive instruction. Boston: Beacon Press

Delpit, L. (2006). Other people's children: Cultural conflict in the classroom. New York: The New Press.

DeRidder, L. M. 1990. "How Suspension and Expulsion Contribute to Dropping Out." *Education Digest* 56: 44–47.

Doyle, J. (2006). Introduction to interviewing techniques. Worcester Polytechnic Institute. Interdisciplinary and Global Studies.

Duncan, G. (2002). Beyond Love: A Critical Race Ethnography of the Schooling of Adolescent Black Males. Equity & Excellence in Education, 35(2):131-143.

Duncan-Andrade, J. M. (2010). *What a coach can teach a teacher: Lessons urban schools can learn from a successful sports program*. Washington, DC: Peter Lang.

Ellison, R. (1995). *Invisible man*. Vintage.

Elsner, A. (2004). Gates of injustice: The crisis in America's prisons. New Jersey: Prentice Hall.

Eisner, E., & Peshkin, A. (1990). *Qualitative inquiry in education: The continuing debate*. New York: Teachers College Press.

Ferguson, A. (2003). Bad boys: *Public schools in the making of black masculinity* . University of Michigan Press.

Ford, D. Y., Grantham, □. C., & Bailey,D. F. (1999). Identifying gifted-ness among African American males :Recommendations □or effective recruitment and retention. In V. C. Polite & J. E. Davis (Eds.),African American males in school and society (pp. 51–67).

Fordham S., Ogbu J. U. (1986). Black students' school success: Coping with the "burden of 'acting white.'" *Urban Review*, 18, 178–206.

Foster, H. L. (1986). Ribbin', jivin', and playin' the dozens: The persistent dilemma in our schools. (2nd ed.). Cambridge, MA: Ballinger.

Foucault, Michel (1977) *Discipline and Punish: The Birth of the Prison*. New York: Pantheon Books.

Freire, P. (1970). Pedagogy of the Oppressed. New York: Herder and Herder.

Gage, N.L. (1989). The paradigm wars and their aftermath: A historical sketch of research on teaching. Educational Researcher, 18)7), 4-10.

Gandara, M. (1995). The racialized actions of Mexican American students. Hispanic Journal of Behavioral Sciences, 19(3), 301-318.

Gardner, H. (1993). *Multiple Intelligences: The Theory in Practice*. New York: Basic Books.

Gay, G. (2000). *Culturally, responsive teaching: Theory, research, & practice*. New York: Teachers College Press.

Glatfelter, Andrew Gary (2006). Substitute Teachers as Effective Classroom Instructors. A Doctoral Dissertation, UCLA.

Gorski, P. (2012): Perceiving the Problem of Poverty and Schooling: Deconstructing the Class Stereotypes that Mis-Shape Education Practice and Policy, Equity & Excellence in Education, 45:2, 302-319

Gramsci, A. (1992). Buttigieg, Joseph A, ed. *Prison Notebooks*. New York City: Columbia University Press. pp. 233–38

Great City Schools Report (2010). A Call for Change: The social and educational factors contributing to the outcomes of Black males in urban schools. Washington, D.C.

Gregory, A. & Thompson, A. (2010). African American high school students and variability in behavior across classrooms. Journal of Community Psychology, 38, 386–402.

Gurian, M. (2007). The Minds of Boys. Jossey-Bass, New York, NY.

Gurion, M., Stevens, K., Henley, P., Trueman,T. (2001). Boys and Girls Learn Differently!A Guide for Teachers and Parents. Jossey-Bass, San Francisco, CA.

Hale, J. (2001). *Learning while Black: Creating educational excellence for African American children.* Baltimore, MD: Johns Hopkins University.

Harris, F. & Bensimon, E. M. (2006). The equity scorecard: A collaborative approach to assess and respond to racial/ethnic disparities in student outcomes. New Directions for Student Services, 2007, 77–84. doi: 10.1002/ss.259

Harry, B. & Klinger, J. (2007). Discarding the Deficit Model, Educational Leadership, 64, 5, pp. 16-21. Retrieved October 9, 2008 from http://findarticles.com/p/articles/mi_qa3614/is_200802/ai_n25137781

Hill, D. (2004) Analysis, Anger and Activism: What Can We Do About It? Autobiography of a socialist activist educator. Rouge Forum documents.

hooks, b. (1981). Ain't I a woman: Black women and feminism. Boston, MA: South End Press.

Hopkins R. (1997). *Educating black males: Critical lessons in schooling, community, and power*. New York: State University of New York Press.

Howard, T.C. (2008). Telling their side of the story: African American students' perceptions of culturally relevant pedagogy. Urban Review, 33(2)

Howard, T. C. (2010). *Why race and culture matters in schools: Closing the achievement gap in America's classrooms*. New York, NY: Teachers College Press.

Howard,T.C. (2013). How does it feel to be a problem? Black male students, schools, and learning in enhancing the knowledge base to disrupt deficit frameworks. Review of Research in Education. 37(1). Pp.54-86.

Hudson, M. J., & Holmes, B. J. (1994). Missing teachers, impaired communities: The unanticipated consequences of Brown v. Board of Education on the African American teaching force at the precollegiate level. *The Journal of Negro Education, 63*, 388-393.

Irvine, J. (1990). *Black students and school failure: Politics, practices, and prescriptions*. New York: Greenwood.

Isom, D. A. (2007). Performance, resistance, caring: Racialized gender identity in African American boys. *Urban Review: Issues and Ideas in Public Education, 39*(4), 405-423.

Kafele, B. K. (2009). Motivating Black Males to Achieve in School and in Life. Alexandria, VA:ASCD.

Kenyatta, C.P. (2012). From Perception to Practice: How Teacher-Student Interactions Affect African American Male Achievement. Temple University.

King,J.E.(1994).The purpose of schooling for African-American children. *Teaching diverse populations: Formulating a knowledge base* (pp. 25-56). Albany, NY: State University of New York Press.

Klem, A. M., & Connell, J. P. (2004). Relationships matter: Linking teacher support to student engagement and achievement. *Journal of School Health, 74*(7), 262-273.

Kozol, J. (2005). *Savage inequalities: Children in America's schools*. New York: HarperPerennial.

Kunjufu, J. (2004). *Countering the conspiracy to destroy Black boys* (Revised/Expanded ed.). Chicago, Ill.: African American Images.

Jackson, J. H. (2010). Yes We Can: The Schott 50 State Report on Public Education and Black Males. Cambridge, MA: The Schott Foundation for Public Education

Jenkins, T. S. (2006). Mr. nigger: The challenges of educating Black males within American society. *Journal of Black Studies*, 37, 127-155.

Johns, T.C. (2008). Telling their side of the story: African American students' perceptions of culturally relevant pedagogy. Urban Review, 33(2)

Lacy, R. 2008. Blue-Chip Black: Race, Class, and Status in the New Black Middle Class. Berkeley: University of California Press.

Ladson-Billings, G. (1994). The Dreamkeepers: Successful teachers of African American children. San Francisco: Jossey-Bass.

Ladson-Billings, G. (2006). From the Achievement Gap to the Education Debt: Understanding Achievement in U. S. Schools. Educational Researcher, 35(7).

Ladson-Billings, G. & Tate, William, F. (2006) 'Towards a Critical Race Theory of Education' in Dixson, A & Rousseau, C. (Eds.) *Critical Race Theory in Education: All God's Children Got a Song*, New York: Routledge Levin, H. (2008). The Economic Payoff to Investing in Educational Justice. *Educational Researcher, 38*(1), 5-20.

Landsman, J., & Lewis, C. (Eds.). (2006). *White teachers/diverse classrooms: A guide to building inclusive schools, promoting high expectations, and eliminating racism.* Sterling, VA: Stylus.

Lewis, C. (2006). African American male teachers in public schools: An examination of three urban school districts. *Teachers College Record, 108*(2), 224-245.

Lewis, C., Hancock, S., James, M., & Larke, P. (2006). African American K-12 students and No Child Left Behind legislation: Progression or digression in educational attainment. *Multicultural Learning & Teaching.*

Lewis, S.; Simon, C.; Uzzell, R.; Horwitz, A.; Cassely, M. 2010. A Call for Change: The Social and Educational Factors Contributing to the Outcomes of Black Males in Urban Schools. Washington, DC: The Council of the Great City Schools.

Linguistic Society of America. (1997). LSA resolution on the Oakland "Ebonics" issue.

Linsin, M. (2012). Why Intimidation is a Terrible Classroom Management Strategy. Smart Classroom Management.

Lorain, P. (2004). Can't Stop Talking: Social Needs of Students in the Middle. National Education Association.

Lunt, P. and S. Livingstone (1996). 'Rethinking the focus group in media and communications research', *Journal of communication* 46(2): 79-98.

Majors, R. & Billson, J. U. (1994). The American Black male: His present status and his future. Chicago: Nelson-Hall.

McCall, Leslie (2005), "The Complexity of Intersectionality," *Signs: Journal of Women in Culture and Society*, 30: 1771-800.

McCadden, B. M. 1998. "Why Is Michael Always Getting Timed Out? Race, Class, and the Disciplining of Other People's Children." In *Classroom Discipline in American Schools: Problems and Possibilities for Democratic Education*, edited by R. E. Butchart and B. McEwan. Albany: State University of New York Press, 109–134.

McDermott, R. P. (1997) Achieving School Failure 1972-1997. In Education and Cultural Process: Anthropological Approaches. 3rd edition. George D. Spindler, ed. Pp. 110-135. Prospect Heights, IL:Waveland.

Milner, H. R. (2006). But good intentions are not enough: Theoretical and philosophical relevance in teaching students of color. In J. Landsman & C. Lewis (Eds.), *White teachers in diverse classrooms: A guide to building inclusive schools, promoting high expectations, and eliminating racism* (pp. 79-90). Sterling, VA: Stylus.

Mishler, E. G. (1979). Meaning in context: Is there any other kind? Harvard Educational Review, 49(1),1-19.

Mitchell, A. (1998). African American teachers: Unique roles and universal lessons. *Education and Urban Society, 31*(1), 104-122.

Montalvo, G. P., Mansfield, E. A., & Miller, R. B. (2007). Liking or disliking the teacher: Student motivation, engagement and achievement. *Evaluation and Research in Education, 20*(3), 144-158.

NAACP. (2005) Interrupting the School to Prison Pipeline. Washington DC.

National Center for Education Statistics. (2013). *National Assessment of Educational Progress: The nation's report card.* Washington, DC: U.S. Department of Education.

National Center for Education Statistics, NAEP 2009 High School Transcript Study," 2009.

Nieto, S. (2009). Affirming Diversity: The Sociopolitical Context of Multicultural Education. (5 ed.) Pearson.

Nittle, N. (2011) What is Race? Debunking the Ideas Behind this Construct. Race Relations. Accessed August 8, 2014.

Noguera, P. (2008). The trouble with Black boys: And other reflections on race, equity, and the future of public education. San Francisco: Jossey-Bass.

Noguera, P. (2012). Saving Black and Latino Boys. Phi Delta Kappa International.

Oakes, J. (2005). Keeping track: How schools structure inequality. (2 ed.). New Haven: Yale University Press.

O'Connor, C., & Fernandez, S. D. (2006). Race, class, and disproportionality: Reevaluating the relationship between poverty and special education placement. *Educational Researcher*, 35(6), 6–11.

Pastorino E., & Doyle S. (2013). What is Psychology? Cengage Learning.

Patton, M. (1990). Qualitative evaluation and research methods (pp. 169-186). Beverly Hills CA:Sage.

Peshkin, A. (1988). In Search of Suvjectivity. One's Own. Educational Researcher 17(7), p.17-21.

Pewewardy, C. D. (1994). Culturally responsible pedagogy in action: An American Indian magnet school. In E. R. Hollins, J. E. King, & W. C. Hayman (Eds.), *Teaching diverse populations: Formulating a knowledge base* (p. 77-92). Albany, NY: State University of New York.

Public Agenda. 2004. "Teaching Interrupted: Do Discipline Policies in Today's Public Schools Foster the Common Good?"

Quiocho, A., & Rios, F. (2000). The power of their presence: Minority group teachers and schooling. *Review of Educational Research, 70*, 485-528.

Richardson, L. (2000). Writing: A method of inquiry. In N. Denzin & Y. Guba (Eds.). *Handbook of qualitative research* (2nd ed., pp. 923-948). Thousand Oaks, CA: Sage.

Riddick, L. (2009). African American Boys in Early Childhood Education (Elementary School) and Understanding the Achievement Gap through the Perceptions of Educators. McNair Scholars Journal, 11:151-186.

Rios, V. (2006) The Hyper-Criminalization of Black and Latino Male Youth in the Era of Mass Incarceration, Souls: A Critical Journal of Black Politics,

Culture, and Society, 8:2, 40-54

Sadker. M. & Sadker, D. (1995). Failing at fairness: how our schools cheat girls. New York: Touchstone.

Salzer, M. S. (2000). Toward a narrative conceptualization of stereotypes: Contextualizing perceptions of public housing residents. *Journal of Community & Applied Social Psychology, 10*(2), 123–137.

Scheurich, J. J. (1993). Toward a white discourse on white racism. *Educational Researcher, 22*(8), 5-10.

Shakespeare, J. (2012). Saving Our Boys: Resetting our Value System. Southern Education Desk.

Shujaa, M.J. (1994). Too Much Schooling, Too Little Education. African World Press.

Skiba, R. J. 2000. "When Is Disproportionality Discrimination? The Overrepresentation of Black Students in School Suspension." In *Zero Tolerance: Resisting the Drive for Punishment in Our Schools*, edited by W. Ayers, B. Dohrn, and R. Ayers. New York: New Press, 176–187.

Sleeter, C. E., & Soriano, E. (2012). Creating Solidarity across Diverse Communities: International Perspectives in Education. New York, NY: Teachers College Press.

Sue, D. W., Bucceri, J., A.I., Nadal, K.L., & Torino, G. (2007). Racial microaggressions and the Asian American experience. Cultural Diversity and Ethnic minority Psychology, 12(1), 72-81.

Teaching Leadership. (2011). Race, Class, and the Achievement Gap: The Promise of Student Potential. Leadership Packet.

The Schott 50 State Report on Public Education and Black Males. 2010. Schott Foundation for Public Education.

Thompson, G.L. (2007). *Up Where We Belong: Helping African American and Latino Students Rise in School and in Life*. San Francisco, CA: Jossey-Bass.

Toldson, I. A. (2013). *Decreasing Dropout Rates for African American Male Youth with Disabilities*. Clemson, SC: National Dropout Prevention Center for Students with Disabilities (NDPC-SD) for the United States Department of Education, Office of Special Education Programs (OSEP).

Toldson, I. A. & Lewis, C.W. (2012). Challenge the Status Quo. Congressional Black Caucus.

Tyre, P. (2008). The trouble with boys. New York, NY: Crown Publishers.

US Department of Education, National Center for Education Statistics. NAEP 2014 Trends in Academic Progress Washington, DC: US Department of Education, August 2014.

Vygotsky, L. (1987). The collected works of L.S. Vygotsky. New York, NY:Plenum Press.

Whitmire, R. (2011). Why boys fail: *Saving our sons from an educational system that's leaving them behind*. AMACOM.

Wooddell, G., & Henry, J. (2005). The advantage of a focus on advantage: A note on teaching minority groups. *Teaching Sociology, 33*(3), 301–309.

U.S. Census Bureau. (2010). *CPS 2010 Annual Social and Economic supplement*. Retrieved from http://www.census.gov/cps/data/cpstablecreator.html

U.S. Department of Education. (2004) Office of Civil Rights Data.

U.S. Department of Education. (2005) Office of Civil Rights Data.
U.S. Department of Education. (2010). Digest of Education Statistics, 2009.
        Washington,
DC: National Center for Education Statistics.
U.S. Department of Justice, Office of Justice Programs, Bureau of Justice Statistics.
        (2014).